PHOTOGRAPHING WATERFOWL

Techniques for the Advanced Amateur and Professional

KIT HOWARD BREEN

VOYAGEUR PRESS

*To father and mother, who first encouraged my
initial efforts as a young photographer.*

*With much appreciation and many thanks to Jan, John, Ron, JoAnn, Bonnie,
and Vicki, whose help and support helped make this book possible.*

Printed in Canada

89 90 91 92 93 5 4 3 2 1

Library of Congress Cataloging-in-Publication Data

Breen, Kit Howard.
   Photographing waterfowl.

   Bibliography: p.
   Includes index.
   1. Photography of birds. I. Title.
TR729.B5B74 1989   778.9'32   89-5536
ISBN 0-89658-096-2 (pbk.)

Published by Voyageur Press Inc.
123 North Second Street
Stillwater, MN 55082 U.S.A.
1-800-888-9653

Voyageur Press books are also available at discounts in bulk quantities for premium or sales-promotion use. For details contact the Marketing Manager.

Please write or call for our free catalog of natural history publications.

COVER: This majestic Canada goose was photographed as it paused to rest while feeding in the shoreline grasses.

ABOVE: The pattern and rhythm of this shot of a flying snow goose family caught my eye. I like the juxtaposition of their wings and the diagonal lines of their formation. (400mm, f/3.5 lens)

PRECEDING PAGE: Canada goslings.

Contents

Windy Woody

Introduction

Why do people photograph waterfowl? Ducks and geese are fun to photograph! They are entertaining to watch, relatively easy to find in the wild, and often more tame than songbirds. Some wild ducks and geese will even eat from your hand. They have a wide variety of interesting behaviors and sometimes engage in the most amusing antics. The courtship ballets of some ducks and grebes are fascinating to watch. And the aerial acrobatics of Canada and snow geese flying in for a landing on very windy days are worthy of a Disney cartoon feature.

Ducks and geese can also be very beautiful. Some have lovely, delicate feather patterns, while others have bright, bold coloring. They are graceful in flight and attractive as they swim lazily along the water. Who can forget the sight and sounds of a crisp morning with the sun rising over a marsh filled with ducks and geese?

This book has been written for the serious photographer who is already familiar with 35mm photography. It presumes knowledge of basics such as use of the camera and light meters, depth of field, and setting of proper exposures. In the chapters that follow, the concentration will be on specific information related to photographing waterfowl: where and when to find ducks and geese, useful equipment for the camera and the photographer, instructions for making blinds, sources of materials for blinds and ready-made blinds, notes on composition and lighting, ideas for creating more artistic photographs, and, finally, suggestions for matting, framing, displaying, and selling your photographs and slides.

For an excellent, comprehensive book covering basic information about nature photography—such as use of the camera, exposure meters, depth of field, filters, films, and so on—I highly recommend John Shaw's *The Nature Photographer's Complete Guide to Professional Field Techniques*.

This wood duck appeared at a small suburban pond surrounded by houses. Normally a very shy duck, this woody followed the tame mallards in for a handout of corn. (300mm f/2.8 lens)

These Canada goslings were photographed within minutes after hatching on an island in a park pond in Virginia. This was taken from a distance of 32 feet (9.7 meters) with a 400mm f/3.5 lens and a 1.4x teleconverter.

1 / Where to Find Ducks, Geese, and Swans

Successful photography of waterfowl requires a population of birds in a natural-looking habitat and some means of getting close to them. Ducks out in the middle of the river a hundred yards or more away can be studied with field glasses, but they cannot be photographed without extremely long (and expensive) telephoto lenses. For close views of one or several birds, a range of 15 to 30 feet (4.5 to 9 meters) is ideal.

To achieve this close a range for your photography, either you must set up your camera in a blind so they cannot see you or you must find a group of birds tame enough to come to you. Chapter 6 describes several types of blinds (or "hides" as they are known in Great Britain) useful for photographing waterfowl in their natural habitat. This chapter will suggest places to find relatively tame wild waterfowl you can photograph at close range. The chapter also includes ideas for finding and photographing captive waterfowl and for dealing with certain limitations, such as clipped wings.

Freshwater Ponds and Lakes

One of the first places to look for tame waterfowl in your area is parks and golf courses with small ponds or lakes. Here will often be found mallards, Canada geese, and sometimes mute swans that are very friendly and tame. Wherever small children can find waterfowl, they are sure to feed them bread, popcorn, crackers, cookies, and the like. The birds seem to be totally undiscriminating about what they will eat, voraciously snapping up whatever they are offered. Happily, they will also eat duck feed and cracked or whole corn, which is what I usually offer them when I feed them.

Mallards and Canada geese are the most commonly found waterfowl in parks. However, other less common species—for example, wood ducks, black ducks, wigeons, teals, redheads, grebes, pintails, and coots—may also be found in local parks, and may gradually become tame as they associate with the mallards and Canadas being fed. The wood duck in the photo was photographed in a small suburban pond surrounded by houses as he followed the mallards in for food.

The unusual species are found more often in winter, when food is in short supply and open water is hard to find due to ice and snow. When some ponds are frozen, others with more swift-moving water may remain open or partially open. Heated water outflow from power plants and industry may also provide open water that will attract waterfowl.

During the spring and summer, local ponds in populated areas of the United States will likely have fewer species. However, nesting mallards, mute swans, and "local" Canada geese (geese that stay year-round in the same location) provide great subjects for photography. Black ducks and wood ducks may also be found nesting throughout much of the U.S. and Canada. "Local" Canada geese do not migrate north, either because they have been injured and cannot fly or because they are descendants of injured birds—goslings born to nonmigrating parents will not migrate. That is why the size of the local Canada geese flocks in parks, on golf courses, and on small ponds continue to grow.

Look for the nests of Canada geese in more isolated spots away from traffic areas. The goslings pictured hatched on a tiny island in the park pond near my home. I was able to photograph them soon after they hatched with my 400mm lens and a 1.4x teleconverter from a distance of 32 feet (9.7 meters).

Mallards are less discriminating than Canada geese when it comes to choosing their nesting site. A friend of mine found a mallard nest beside her back door in plain sight under a rose bush. A small

Young mallard duckling found at a local pond. This shot was taken from a distance of 8 feet (2.4 meters) with a 180mm f/2.8 lens.

Open patches of water in frozen rivers make fine "duck traps." This canvasback duck was lured close in with corn. (300mm f/2.8 lens)

stream behind my townhouse with a busy pathway nearby was the home for another mallard brood one spring. Still another family of mallards made headlines one day when they stopped traffic on Pennsylvania Avenue two blocks from the nation's Capitol Building, as mother led her young ducklings across the road to water. It is even rumored in Washington that some of the local mallard ducks have security clearances! Each summer for the past seven years, several families of mallards have been raised inside the center courtyard of the Pentagon.

Salt Water

If you live near a tidal river or saltwater estuary, there will be many other species to photograph in the fall and winter. Loons, for example, may be found in the rivers off the Chesapeake Bay in October and November. Canvasbacks (ponchards), oldsquaws (long-tailed ducks), goldeneyes, buffleheads, redheads, ring-necked ducks, blue- and green-winged teals, and scaup are often seen in salt water bays and rivers in winter.

In the Puget Sound area of Washington and the Fraser River Delta near Vancouver, British Columbia, a great number of waterfowl spend the winter in the waters warmed by the Humbold Current. Species that may be found here in winter include harlequin ducks, green-winged teal, shovelers, Western grebes, Barrow's goldeneyes, gadwalls, scaup, scoters, hooded and common mergansers, trumpeter and tundra swans, and several species of geese.

The problem, of course, is how to find waterfowl close enough for photographing. One possibility in cold winters is finding open pockets of water near shore when the rivers or lakes are mostly frozen. One very cold winter, there was such a pocket of open water in the Tred Avon River, Maryland. The open area was behind a small jetty covered with ice chunks. By stretching out on the ice chunks on the shoreline, I was partially hidden by the jetty. Corn thrown onto the ice near the edge of the open water brought several canvasback ducks in close enough for a good shot.

During the winter, piers and pilings at marinas are good places to find bay ducks close to shore. Oldsquaws, for example, like to feed on the barnacles or seaweed on pilings. They swim up and down an area of pilings, diving occasionally for food. When I spot an oldsquaw working a dock for food, I watch its direction of travel from a distance. Then as the duck dives under to feed, I run up closer to where I anticipate it will surface. Usually,

to minimize my visibility, I stretch out on the pier or ground with my camera on the lowest tripod setting, ready to snap the shot as the duck surfaces. If I remain completely still while the duck is on the surface, I can usually work my way in quite close to it.

A less strenuous method of finding wild ducks in saltwater close enough to photograph is to make use of tame mallards as living decoys. At Oxford, Maryland, for example, there is a large flock of town ducks that hang out near the ferryboat slip. These mallards are regularly fed in winter by local townspeople as well as by casual visitors. As a result, the area often attracts more unusual species in winter. Canvasbacks, blue-winged teals, goldeneyes, redheads, and of course the ubiquitous coot, as well as mute and tundra swans, may be seen here on occasion. These visitors join in with the mallards to feast on the free corn. The blue-winged teal's photo was taken at this location one winter.

Some of my best photographs of wild waterfowl have been taken with the kind cooperation of local waterfowl enthusiasts who have flocks they regularly feed in winter. Along the Chesapeake Bay, I have met a number of people who feed geese or swans that congregate near their homes on the bay. Apparently, once a migrating flock of geese or swans has become accustomed to being fed, they return year after year to the same place, bringing their offspring with them. Photographing in this kind of situation, of course, requires permission to be on private property. And sometimes it requires that the birds' regular feeder be present, as they may not trust any stranger who offers them corn. It may also be important to know the time of day the birds are usually fed, for they may not come around at any other time. The tundra swans pictured were close enough for me to photograph only because they had just eaten corn from the kind gentleman who owned the dock on which I was standing.

From the standpoint of waterfowl conservation, supplemental feeding in the winter has its pros and cons. People who love waterfowl often want to feed them. Around the Chesapeake Bay and, I imagine, elsewhere in the country where ducks gather, a number of people feed ducks and geese regularly. A neighbor on Kent Island, for example, regularly feeds whole corn to "his flock" of ducks, geese, and swans during the winter. Some of the same banded swans return to his property every year. On the one hand, the birds he feeds have an easy time getting nutritious food through his efforts. That leaves more natural food for the others in the vicinity. On the other hand, if he stops feeding his winter flock, they may have difficulty finding other food sources. I have seen small suburban ponds overrun with many more ducks than the natural food supply can support. This happens sometimes when people fairly regularly supplement their food. Small children love to feed ducks in the parks and who can blame them? I still am delighted when a wild creature takes food from my hand.

When I do offer food to waterfowl to entice them closer for photographs, I use whole or cracked corn whenever possible since that is a common food for geese in the Chesapeake region. If the water is so deep that the corn sinks below the level they can reach, I sometimes substitute whole-grain bread because it floats. But I use the bread reluctantly and sparingly because I know it is not especially good for them.

State Wildlife Management Areas

Food for waterfowl is increasingly less and less plentiful as their natural feeding grounds are converted to farms or subdivisions. Where states have set aside land for raising crops for waterfowl feed and built marshes and ponds for them, you are likely to find good places for photography. Some of the state wildlife management areas allow hunting. And some have limited access at certain times of the year, such as during nesting season. Check with your local state wildlife conservation authority for information on state-managed waterfowl refuges where photography might be possible.

National Wildlife Refuges

The national wildlife refuges administered by the U.S. Department of the Interior number more than 380. These vary tremendously in habitat and size, some being marsh and wetlands, others desert, still others mountain or prairie lands set aside for the protection of endangered plants and animals. The very first of these refuges was established under the administration of Teddy Roosevelt in 1903 on tiny Pelican Island in Florida. Some have been established primarily to protect animals, for example, the National Bison Range, the National Elk Refuge, and the Sheldon Antelope Refuge. Other refuges have a variety of habitat with many kinds of plants, animals, and birds. Still others are primarily wetlands set aside for waterfowl wintering or nesting sites.

Among those refuges with good concentrations of waterfowl, a few are outstanding for their photographic opportunities. For a complete listing and description of all the national wildlife refuges, Laura and William Riley's *Guide to the National Wildlife Refuges* (1979) is indispensable—an excellent, comprehensive guide to the refuges. This book describes the habitat, lists the creatures found there, gives accurate directions for getting to the refuge, and even tells the best times to visit. It also indicates which refuges have photographic blinds in place.

What the guide does not tell you is which refuges are more likely to be suitable for good waterfowl photography. My experiences with some twenty or so waterfowl-oriented refuges across the United States have been mixed. In some refuges I visited, the birds were quite far away from the visitors' areas, so that it was impossible to get good photographs. I have listed below several refuges that my friends and I have found productive for waterfowl photography. This is by no means an exhaustive listing. There may be others we have not seen that are better.

The following are a few national wildlife refuges with "cooperative" waterfowl:

> Bosque Del Apache, New Mexico
> snow geese, sandhill cranes, whooping cranes, Canada geese, seventeen species of ducks;
> National Elk Refuge, Wyoming
> trumpeter swans, seven species of ducks;
> Des Lacs, North Dakota
> grebes, many species of ducks, sandhill cranes, tundra swans;
> Horicon, Wisconsin
> Canada geese, blue-winged teal, redheads, ruddy ducks;
> Brigantine, New Jersey
> brants, snow geese, Canada geese, blue- and green-winged teals, pintails, shovelers;
> Bombay Hook, Delaware
> Canada geese, snow geese, pintails, wigeons, scaup, mergansers, blue-winged teals, buffleheads;
> Chincoteague, Virginia
> brants, snow geese, Canada geese, shovelers, gadwalls, wigeons, pintails, buffleheads;
> Mattamuskeet, North Carolina
> tundra swans, pintails, eleven other species of ducks.

The oldsquaw was diving for food around pilings at a local marina. I was able to snap this shot soon after he surfaced from a dive. (400mm f/3.5 lens)

The blue-winged teal was preening himself after a meal of corn shared with his mallard companions. (300mm f/4.5 lens, hand held)

Tundra swans settling a dispute. These swans come daily to this spot on the shoreline of the Chesapeake Bay for corn. The same birds return each winter to feed at this man's property. (300 f/4.5 lens)

Children of all ages like to feed ducks and geese. This often provides good opportunities for the patient photographer.

This wild gadwall and his mate spent a few weeks in winter at the zoo duck pond where the water was kept open and the food was plentiful. By standing very still at the edge of the pond, I was able to get this shot as he cruised by me. (400 f/3.5 lens)

Canadian areas with waterfowl concentrations:*
  Fraser Estuary, Reifel Refuge, Vancouver, B.C.
    trumpeter and tundra swans, snow geese, many species of ducks, especially in winter, but some breeding ducks also;
  Stanley Park, Vancouver, B.C.
    Western grebes, harlequin ducks, Barrow's goldeneyes, green-winged and cinnamon teals, wood ducks;
  Delta Marsh, Portage la Prairie, Manitoba
    snow geese, white-fronted geese, Ross's geese during migration, scaup, mergansers, many species of nesting ducks;
  Oak Hammock Marsh, Winnipeg, Manitoba
    similar to Delta Marsh.

In general, the refuges with large numbers of visitors seem more productive for waterfowl photography than those that have few visitors. I have observed that the less-frequented refuges, especially those that allow hunting, have more skittish and wary bird populations. By contrast, the ducks and geese at frequently visited refuges, being more accustomed to people, are more likely to remain near the wildlife drives and visitor areas, posing for photographers.

Waterfowl in Zoos

Turning now from wild waterfowl to captive waterfowl—what can be said for waterfowl photography in a zoo? Some purists may sneer at the idea of photographing any creature in a zoo. However, a zoo or other captive waterfowl population allows you to photograph things you might not otherwise find without a great deal of difficulty. Zoo birds, being used to people, will tolerate very close-range photography. Furthermore, the zoo may well attract wild waterfowl seeking an easy food supply and open water in the winter. The pictured wild gadwall and his mate spent several months at the National Zoo before departing in the spring. While I have seen gadwalls at national wildlife refuges, I have never been able to get a close shot of one there. The wild birds in associating with the more tame zoo birds gradually become more tolerant of people, allowing me to obtain shots such as this with a 300mm lens.

There are, of course, disadvantages to photographing captive birds. To prevent the birds from flying away, usually one wingtip is clipped. Several prominent wing feathers will be visibly missing in clipped ducks or geese. With care, however, one can photograph ducks on the side opposite the clipped wing. In fast-action shots, the clipped wing will not be evident.

Another problem with photographing in a zoo may be poor backgrounds and greenish, muddy brown, or black-looking water. The water at the D.C. National Zoo often appears green because of algae and the reflection of the many trees surrounding the shallow ponds.

My favorite times for zoo photography are winter and early spring. I try to visit early in the morning on less crowded weekdays. By standing or sitting very still with my camera ready, and moving very slowly when I change positions, I can often get closeup shots even of the less tame wild visitors. Quick movements or people's walking past sends the ducks to the furthest edges of the ponds, especially the wild visitors.

Duck "Farmers" and Rehabilitators

In conclusion, I should mention another resource for good closeup photographs of captive ducks and geese: the waterfowl "farmers" and rehabilitators. Ducks and geese being cared for by these people will generally be in closed pens with wire or netting over the top to prevent flight or attack by hawks and owls.

Wildlife rehabilitators are trained volunteers who care for sick and injured wildlife at their homes. Many rehabilitators and organizations concerned with protection of wildlife belong to the National Wildlife Rehabilitators Association, RR 1, Box 125E, Brighton, Illinois 62012. Another source for names of waterfowl rehabilitators is your local Audubon Society. All the rehabilitators I have met have been friendly, dedicated people who are knowledgeable about the creatures they rescue, and they are always willing to help with an injured bird or animal. (I have carried a small pair of wire cutters in my camera case ever since I found a baby gosling entangled in fish hooks and wire.)

In addition to the rehabilitators, a variety of people raise wild species of ducks and geese for conservation or for sale. Some of these sell ducks to zoos and to decoy carvers. Several of the professional decoy carvers have ponds with their own collection of ducks. Information about these duck "farmers" is available at wildfowl shows and festivals. Decoy carvers are likely to know who raises ducks in their area.

*Findlay, J.C. *A Bird-Finding Guide to Canada*. Edmonton, Alberta: Aspen House, 1984.

This early morning view of Canada geese in the grass illustrates the soft golden color of the light soon after sunrise. (300mm f/4.5 lens)

Canada geese often leave their daytime feeding and resting grounds to fly out on the water for the night. "Geese Over Dock" was taken near sunset on a foggy afternoon. This is the color of the scene with a telephoto lens. No filter was used. (300mm f/4.5 lens)

2 / When to Photograph Waterfowl

Time of Day

Waterfowl are most active and best photographed from sunrise to early morning and from midafternoon to sunset. Not only are the birds more alert and active but the lighting is much better in these hours. Midday lighting tends to be harsh and overbright for photography. The softer, more golden light near sunrise and sunset can make the whole photograph. The shot of early morning geese, for example, would not be nearly as effective or interesting if taken at midday. It is the quality of the golden sidelighting on the grasses and geese contrasting with the bright blue water that is appealing here. The photograph was taken about an hour after sunrise.

Hunters know that geese often sleep at night on the water, then soon after sunrise fly to land some distance away to feed. They may return to water at times during the day, particularly if they are thirsty from feeding in a dry field. Goose hunters' blinds are often set up in the middle of cornfields or beside freshwater ponds. The hunters are usually in place in their blinds before sunup.

Near sunset, geese leave the land and fly to a safe haven on the water for the night, except during the full moon. Knowing this enabled me to catch a flock of Canada geese flying to the water one foggy afternoon at sunset. I had set up my camera on a tripod near where the geese were feeding, calculating their flight direction so that the sun was over my shoulder. I was fortunate that the wind was coming from the desired direction, as geese and ducks nearly always take off directly into the wind.

Days with colorful sunsets offer an opportunity for interesting silhouette shots of flying geese. If you know where the geese are likely to fly at sun-

set, you can position yourself so they will fly between you and the setting sun. Of course, they may not cooperate the day you are waiting for them. Sometimes they delay their flight to water until the light is fading.

Midday photography on sunny days is difficult due to the strong, often glaring overhead light. Use of a polarizing filter helps cut the glare for scenic shots. Polarizing filters for lenses up to 180mm or 200mm are reasonable in price. For longer lenses, however, filters of any kind are impractical. Not only are they very costly, but they also so greatly reduce the light that stopping action with moving subjects is impossible with anything but the fastest films.

On cloudy days, however, midday may be the best time for taking pictures, from the standpoint of lighting. On bright but clouded days, the lighting is more even, eliminating problems with dark shadows. Since film cannot handle extreme contrasts well, what appears to your eye as pale shadows on your bird may well turn out on the slides to be quite dark. Remember when shooting on cloudy days that birds on the water require special care to handle the light-grey-to-white color reflected off the water. On blue-sky days, shooting toward the water, I generally open up ⅓ to ⅔ of a stop beyond what the light meter reads to accommodate the bright light reflected from the water. But on cloudy days, 1 stop to 1⅓ stops open may be needed when shooting subjects with light grey sky reflected water.

Time of the Month

The time of the month is important to take into account when photographing geese. Hunters

Wood ducks are shy, timid creatures. Conditions must be just right even with "tame" wood ducks to get close enough for shots such as this. (300mm f/2.8 lens)

recognize that their prospects for success are reduced around the time of the full moon. When the moonlight is bright at night, the geese begin to party. They stay up late at night, feasting and flying around in the moonlight, then sleep in late the following day!

Weather Conditions and Waterfowl

A friend has called to tell you a flock of wood ducks have been seen on the pond near his home. It has been raining for two days and will be clearing tomorrow. An ideal time to photograph those woodies? Most likely not. I made that mistake one day, eager to get my shots of the wood ducks. The woodies were on the pond as reported, but I could not get anywhere within camera range of them because of the wind. On windy days waterfowl are nervous

and easily spooked. The wood ducks would not be enticed with food, nor would they remain still on the banks as I slowly approached them. Windy days are not good for close photos of either wild or tame waterfowl. Even zoo birds are more difficult to approach on windy days.

The next day, however, was calm, warmer and quiet. The wood ducks relaxed, swam in close for food, and settled on the bank nearby, allowing me to approach them to within 20 feet (6 meters).

High-wind days do offer the possibility for photographing unusual flight behavior as ducks and geese descend for a landing. In an area where a number of waterfowl are gathered together and landing space is tight, on windy days you may see them "whiffling" as they land. Whiffling, or "maple leafing" as it is sometimes called, occurs as the birds

Windy days offer the possibility for shots of "whiffling" geese and ducks as they descend for a landing. They twist and turn, spilling the air from their wings, dropping a dozen or more feet before spreading their wings to break the fall. (400mm f/3.5 lens)

are descending from a height. They twist and turn, spilling the air from their wings, dropping rapidly a dozen or more feet at a time, before spreading their wings again to break the fall. This behavior is apparently done to control their landing when winds would tend to blow them off course. Some people believe that the young birds whiffle just for the fun of it. This unusual sight is a real challenge to capture on film, and certainly amusing to watch.

Windy days are also good for panning shots of birds as they glide in for a landing. For this type of shot, you must be parallel to their takeoff and landing route. Usually ducks and geese take off and land directly into the wind just like airplanes. If you can position yourself in the right place, you may be able to photograph some interesting flight patterns. When there is little or no wind, waterfowl take off and fly directly away from whatever disturbs them.

Inclement weather, especially the colder days of winter, may not be the most comfortable time to be outdoors, but such days often have rewards for the hardy photographer. Snow or ice in the pond or river can provide an interesting backdrop, hiding unsightly shorelines. And when it is cold enough that most ponds and rivers are frozen over, there will be large concentrations of waterfowl on whatever open water they can find. Furthermore, in such extreme conditions, the birds are likely to be hungry and more willing to swim in close for corn. Some of my best photos are taken on cold icy days. (See Chapter 3, Equipment, for ideas about keeping both cameras and photographer functioning well in harsh conditions.)

A light snowfall lends interest to this shot of a mallard taken at a local pond. It was taken from under the cover of a space blanket used as a tarpaulin to keep the snow off the camera equipment. (400mm f/3.5 lens)

Foggy days are one of my favorite times for photography. The soft outlines, the even lighting and—most of all—the mood evoked by the fog set the scene for some exciting waterfowl photography. (300mm f/2.8 lens)

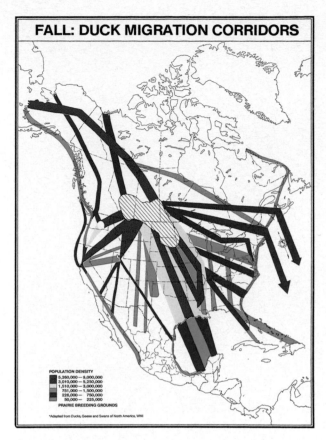

FALL: DUCK MIGRATION CORRIDORS

POPULATION DENSITY
5,260,000 — 9,000,000
3,010,000 — 5,250,000
1,510,000 — 3,000,000
751,000 — 1,500,000
226,000 — 750,000
50,000 — 225,000
PRAIRIE BREEDING GROUNDS

*Adapted from Ducks, Geese and Swans of North America, WMI

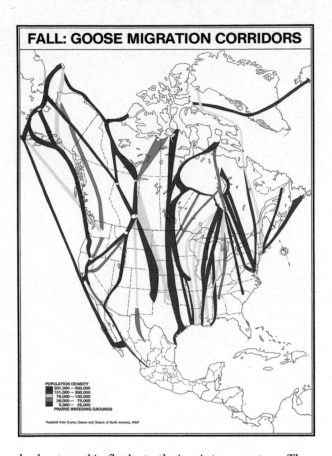

FALL: GOOSE MIGRATION CORRIDORS

POPULATION DENSITY
301,000 — 500,000
151,000 — 300,000
76,000 — 150,000
26,000 — 75,000
5,000 — 25,000
PRAIRIE BREEDING GROUNDS

*Adapted from Ducks, Geese and Swans of North America, WMI

Stormy days make photography even more difficult and uncomfortable. Nonetheless, for the dedicated enthusiast, the possibility exists for some interesting photos of ducks and geese in light snow. The photo of a mallard in snow was taken from the edge of a small pond partially frozen over. Both camera and I were covered with a space blanket used as a tarpaulin.

Foggy days are one of my favorite times for photography. The soft outlines of trees and grasses, the even lighting, and—most of all—the mood evoked by fog set the scene for some exciting waterfowl shots. Scenic and medium-range photographs of groupings of birds are effective in heavy fog or mist.

Waterfowl Seasons of the Year

Fall Migration

A faint honking in the distance, gradually coming closer, and great undulating V's in the sky herald the return of the Canada geese from their northern nesting grounds. What a thrilling spectacle to see masses of geese winging in from the north! Canada geese, snow geese, tundra swans, and white-fronted geese, as well as numerous species of ducks, travel in flocks to their winter quarters. They move along the four major flyways: down the Chesapeake on the Atlantic Flyway, to the Mississippi Delta on the Mississippi Flyway, down across the plains states in the Central Flyway, and down the Pacific coastal states on the Pacific Flyway.

A few weeks prior to the fall migration, ducks and geese begin to mass in staging areas across Canada and in the very northern sections of the United States near the Canadian border. In the Pacific area, the Fraser River delta across from Vancouver Island is a major gathering point for ducks and geese. In the prairie provinces of Alberta and Saskatchewan, the prairie lakes, such as the Quill lakes, and the large river deltas to the north are great staging areas. In Manitoba, the marshes and lakes near Winnepeg contain tremendous numbers of waterfowl. To the east, the tidal flats of the Maritime provinces are major departure points for snow geese and a number of duck species.

Because of the large concentrations of birds, the fall migration is a great time for photography. Depending on weather conditions, temperature, wind direction, and who-knows-what other criteria, the waterfowl begin moving from the Canadian staging areas south into the United States

Mallards up. Ducks are nervous and easily spooked into flight during the hunting season, so I avoid all areas where hunters are likely to be. National wildlife refuges, where hunting is prohibited, are the best places for photography at this time. (400mm f/5.6 lens)

early in September. The first arrivals often appear after a major frontal system has blown through, coasting in on clearing northwest winds.

For information of actual arrival dates, the national wildlife refuge (NWR) personnel record the bird count on their refuges weekly. A telephone call to your nearest refuge will often give you the count for that day. Also useful are the visitor logs maintained by the NWR visitor centers for people to note what unusual species they have seen, where, and when. A glance at the recent log entries will alert you to special finds you might see while touring the refuge.

The warm sunny days of early autumn are relaxing and comfortable to both photographer and waterfowl; however, later in the fall, when hunting is underway, the waterfowl are more nervous and liable to take flight at the slightest provocation. Ducks are especially easily scared into flight. Alarmed pintails, mallards, and teals will take flight much ahead of the geese.

During hunting season, I avoid those areas where hunters are likely to be. It is important to know the hunting seasons for various ducks, doves, geese, quail, and deer in your locale before going into the field to photograph. Wildlife refuges and private sanctuaries where hunting is prohibited are the best places for photography during the hunting season. Ducks and geese know where they are safe from hunters. They fly high over the hunted areas on their way to rest and feed in the safe havens. Photographers should heed their wisdom!

Late in October and November is the time for most of the late migrants to arrive at their wintering grounds. Tundra swans, for example, usually appear on the Chesapeake a full month after the first Canadas have arrived. Bay and sea ducks move south much later than the geese. Loons, for example, feed in the mouths of the rivers along the Chesapeake Bay in early November on their way south to Florida and the Gulf Coast. That is also the time to find canvasbacks, scaup, and redheads on the Chesapeake, as they drift south along the coast to Florida.

On the Pacific Flyway, ducks and geese migrate somewhat more slowly south down through Oregon to California than their cousins migrating on the Central and Mississippi Flyways. Peak waterfowl numbers at the Klamath Basin national wildlife refuges in Oregon and California occur in late October and November. At the Sacramento, California NWR, there may be very few waterfowl gathered before late November or December. And several of the coastal refuges in the Seattle area, such as Nisqually NWR and Dungeness NWR, are winter quarters to many species of bay and sea ducks as well as loons, grebes, and brant ("divers, grebes, and brent," as the British call them).

In the Midwest, the migration of geese and ducks is well underway by early October. How soon the waterfowl leave their staging areas in Canada has a lot to do with the cold weather and freezing of the ponds and marshes. Horicon NWR in eastern Wisconsin has its peak concentration of more than 100,000 Canada geese in October.

Winter

Winter has its own special rewards for the hardy waterfowl photographer. Frost on the grasses in early morning, ice skimming the ponds and rivers, snow, and ice chunks can add interest to your scenics and to your close-ups of waterfowl. Snow and ice will often turn unattractive muddy riverbanks or dull brown water into beautiful settings for a photograph. I like snow cover because it simplifies the background, covering up the clutter.

On the negative side, however, it is often tricky to find your quarry in the winter. Your favorite spot, teeming with waterfowl last week or even yesterday, may be totally barren if the water has frozen up. I went to Bombay Hook NWR in Delaware very early one January. The shallow ponds were mostly frozen closed and there were four inches (ten centimeters) of new snow on the ground. I found a large flock of Canada geese and several dozen snow geese resting in a field beside the entry road on that very cold, windy afternoon. Early the next morning, it was ten degrees Fahrenheit and foggy. I returned to the refuge hoping to get some sunrise photographs, only to find that all the geese had disappeared. The refuge manager thought they had gone further south. There was not a single bird to be seen on the refuge that day other than a hawk and a few cold songbirds.

When the ponds and rivers are frozen closed, the waterfowl move to find open water. They can get along a few days without food, but they must have water. Find the pockets of open water and you will find concentrations of waterfowl. In Canada, the larger alkaline lakes freeze later than the shallow fresh marshes. Deeper ponds with swift moving water will stay open longer than shallow, quiet ponds. Areas of current eddies in rivers are more likely to be open than the shallow coves with little current. Deep water around pilings, docks, and ferryboat slips may stay open longer. Rivers or lakes with warm water effluent from industry or atomic power plants are another possibility for open water that may attract waterfowl.

Midwinter, when the ponds are frozen, is the time to find unusual wild species of ducks camping out in your local zoo ponds. Zoos keep flowing water going into their duck ponds to keep them from freezing. The National Zoo in the District of Columbia has had black ducks, wood ducks, American wigeon, green- and blue-winged teal, pintails, and occasionally a wild gadwall visiting its ponds for food and open water in the winter.

In saltwater locations, some of the water in marinas may be kept open by bubbler systems to protect docks and boats. Check open areas for diving ducks such as oldsquaws ("long-tailed ducks," as the British call them), canvasbacks (ponchards), goldeneyes, and scaup. These are some of the more challenging ducks to photograph in the winter.

Spring

The spring migration is not nearly as spectacular as the fall migration. The large numbers of birds gathered together before the flight appear mainly in the fall. In the spring, the migration appears to be more spread out, with smaller flocks heading north over many days.

Spring is the time for interesting shots of courtship behavior, with male ducks displaying their

Ruddy duck stretching. The ruddy duck male sports a bright-blue bill and chestnut sides and back for the spring courtship. His winter plumage is rather dull. (400mm f/3.5 lens)

most colorful plumage as they dance and preen to attract the females' attention. Several species of ducks have a decidedly different appearance in the spring. The ruddy duck male, for example, sports a bright-blue bill and chestnut-colored side and back feathers in the spring. In the winter he looks rather drab.

In the middle and northern sections of the United States, mallards, black ducks, wood ducks, gadwalls, blue-winged teals, and grebes will be courting and nest building in early spring. In the prairie pothole country of the U.S. and southern Canada, blue- and green-winged teal (cinnamon teal in the far West), canvasbacks, pintails, redheads, ruddy ducks, and several species of grebes will be nesting. Loons will be nesting in Canada and the northern U.S. from northern Minnesota through New York, New Hampshire, and Maine in large ponds and lakes. Trumpeter swans nest in Wyoming and Montana.

Summer

Early summer is, of course, the time to photograph goslings and ducklings. Your local wildlife refuges can tell you what species may be nesting there and whether the area is open to visitors. Mallards and local Canada geese may be found nesting almost anywhere in the middle latitudes of the United States and Canada. Wood ducks are much less numerous, but they do nest in remote wooded areas from the East Coast west through the Mississippi River marshlands to the West Coast.

The prairie states and Canadian prairie provinces have a wealth of colorful nesting ducks in potholes and wetlands. Species to be found in these areas include blue- and green-winged teals; cinnamon teals in the far West; redheads; ruddy ducks; wigeons; shovelers; pintails; gadwalls; eared, horned, and western grebes; and Canada geese.

By midsummer, the ducklings and goslings are growing into adolescents. The adults have gone into the molt stage, losing all their flight feathers at once. This is an exceedingly vulnerable time for the waterfowl because for several weeks they are unable to fly. They generally hide during this stage in remote areas.

By late summer, the ducks and geese have grown new feathers and are fattening up in preparation for the long migratory flight. Some of the ducks are quite unattractive in late summer, especially the mallards. Their scruffy appearance does not lend itself to colorful photographs in late summer or early fall.

The spring courtship dance of Western grebes is a fascinating display. At the conclusion of this elaborate ritual, the two grebes run across the top of the water, carrying weeds in their bills. (400mm f/5.6 lens)

Late April or early May is the time to photograph Canada goslings. They are the first waterfowl to hatch in the spring. (180mm f/2.8 lens)

This "scenic" shot of black ducks in the fog is a good example of the kind of shot one can take with the 105mm f/2.8 lens.

Canada goose feeding. The 180mm f/2.8 lens is ideal for closeup portrait shots of waterfowl.

3 / Equipment for Waterfowl Photography

Basic Equipment—Starting Simply

To begin waterfowl photography it is not necessary to have a lot of expensive equipment. A 35mm camera with a 180mm or 200mm lens plus a tripod will enable you to take closeup photographs of tame ducks and geese as well as fine scenic shots with waterfowl. Your 200mm telephoto can be either a macro lens, a zoom lens, or a regular telephoto lens. For some scenic shots, you may want to use a 50mm or a short telephoto in the 70mm to 105mm range. The shot of black ducks in the fog was taken with a 105mm lens.

If you do not already own a telephoto lens and plan to purchase one for waterfowl and wildlife photography, there are several important points to bear in mind when choosing a lens. If you are buying a 180mm or 200mm lens, the faster the lens is, the more versatile it will be. The faster the lens (i.e., the lower the number of its f-stops), the better it will handle low-light conditions at sunrise and sunset. Furthermore, you will want to use the slower films like Kodachrome 64, Ektachrome 100, or Fujichrome 50 and 100 to avoid excessive grain; so to stop action, freezing moving wings and quacking bills, you will need a shutter speed of 1/500 second. In average bright sunlight with a subject lighted from the front, at 1/500 second you will be shooting at f/5.6 with Kodachrome 64 film.

A 200mm lens will work in this situation for one bird or several birds on the same plane to the camera. However, at f/5.6, your lens will be almost wide open, so focusing will be critical. The depth of field 15 feet (4.5 meters) away from your subject is only 24 inches (61.5 centimeters); at 30 feet (9 meters), the depth of field increases to nearly 8 feet (2.4 meters), according to tables published by Nikon.

The 200mm f/4 is therefore a workable lens with K64 film for both close-in and more distant shots of single birds, or several birds on the same plane with the camera. However, if you wish to add a 2x teleconverter to this lens in order to increase its focal length, you run into problems using K64 film trying to stop action with moving subjects. The 2x teleconverter doubles the focal length from 200mm to 400mm, but it also doubles the lens f-stop to f/8. The speed for correct exposure with Kodachrome 64 in average bright sunlight at f/8 is 1/250 second. Anything less than 1/500 second will not freeze action on close-by subjects.

A faster lens in this range, like the 180mm f/2.8, might be a better choice. The Canada goose photo was taken with a 180mm lens at close range using Kodachrome 64. Using a 2x teleconverter to double an f/2.8 180mm lens gives an effective focal length of 360mm at f/5.6. This faster lens in combination with a 2x teleconverter gives a little more latitude to use slower films. The 2.8 lens also has an advantage in low-light conditions.

The 2x teleconverter is a less expensive way to increase your focal length capability. There is some loss of sharpness in using a teleconverter, however. For many purposes, this loss of crispness should not be troublesome. The exception might be using the slide for large prints, 11 x 14 or 16 x 20 for example, or for publication. The teleconverter will cost much less than a 400mm lens. It is also small and light, a real bonus if you are carrying equipment any distance.

For lenses longer than 200mm there is a 1.4x teleconverter available from several manufacturers. Some professional wildlife photographers use the 1.4x teleconverter rather than the 2x teleconverter with their longer telephoto lenses. It gives less distortion to the image than the 2x teleconverter and it increases the f-stop by a factor of 1.4 instead of 2. The photo of the mallards was taken with a 400mm f/3.5 lens plus a 1.4x teleconverter.

The tripod for your basic outfit for waterfowl photography should be a sturdy, good-quality one that will not be shaken in the wind. It should plant its feet firmly on the ground, giving a steady platform for photographs taken from near ground level. Buying an inexpensive, poorly made tripod is not a good investment. A better choice is to buy the best-made and heaviest one you can reasonably afford and carry. See the section "Tripods and Other Supports" for further discussion of tripod features.

More Sophisticated Camera Equipment

If you are concerned about obtaining the very best possible quality for your photographic images, or if you plan to use them for publication, you should stick to a camera and lenses from a major manufacturer such as Canon, Leica, Minolta, Nikon, or Olympus. Buy the matching lenses from your camera manufacturer, and buy fixed-focal-length lenses rather than zoom lenses. Besides assuring the quality of your lenses, you will have equipment that is designed to work together, and equipment that works consistently from one lens to another. The fixed-focal-length lenses will be faster than zoom lenses, enabling you to use slower, finer-grained film.

If you plan to add a teleconverter, use it only when absolutely necessary. Buy the brand to fit your camera in the 1.4x version for the specific lenses you will use with it. Less expensive teleconverters will not be as sharp as those made by the major manufacturers.

As you look at the array of lenses available in the telephoto range, you will find several choices at each focal length. One choice you will make is the speed, or lowest f-stop, of the lens. I suggest buying the fastest lens you can afford, taking into consideration the size and weight of the lens, especially if you plan to hike with it. If price is no barrier, you still may not wish to buy the fastest lens available because of its weight. For example, a 300mm f/4.5 lens weighs around 2 pounds 6 ounces (1.1 kilograms); a 300mm f/2.8 lens weighs around 5 pounds 4 ounces (2.4 kilograms). The f/4 or f/4.5 300mm lens can easily be hand held with practice. The larger, heavier 300mm f/2.8 lens should be supported on a tripod or monopod. The faster lens is also much larger, some 11 inches (28 centimeters)

long and nearly 6 inches (15 centimeters) in diameter at the front. (Nikon's literature claims that the 300mm 2.8 lens can be hand held. That may be practical shooting at 1/1000 second for brief periods of time, but one certainly cannot hand hold a lens that heavy for very long.) The photograph of the three flying geese was taken with a 300mm f/4.5 lens supported on a bean bag on the car window.

Faster-Focusing Lenses

Another factor to consider in buying your telephoto lens concerns the construction of the lens and its mechanism for focusing. Canon calls its fast focusing "Vari-Pitch Cam" focusing. Nikon calls its version "Internal Focusing" (IF lenses). Lenses with these more expensive quick-focusing mechanisms turn more easily for focusing on moving subjects. It is easier to follow focus on a swimming or flying bird with these fast-focusing lenses. They cost more but I think the added investment is well worthwhile for wildlife photography.

The higher priced fast-focusing telephoto lenses also have a special type of glass for extra low dispersion of colors that increases their sharpness and color balance. Canon calls this type of glass UD for ultra-low dispersion, Nikon ED for extra-low dispersion. This glass helps both sharpness and color correction in lenses 180mm or longer. One can certainly take fine photographs without this more expensive option, but if you want the best possible rendition, buy your telephoto lenses with this type of glass.

Autofocus Cameras

In 1987 and 1988, the major camera manufacturers have concentrated on marketing their version of the automatic focusing camera. The earliest models were primarily aimed at the amateur camera buff and most were apparently rushed into production before the bugs were thoroughly worked out. Camera repair shops report numerous problems with the earliest autofocus cameras. By the summer of 1988, a second generation of autofocus cameras began to appear. The Nikon 8008 is reputed to be a vast improvement over Nikon's earlier autofocus model, in terms of both its capabilities and its expected rate of failure. This model has an optional special back that allows for preselection of a focal distance, with the automatic shutter firing as the subject enters the area of focus. The newest Nikon professional camera, the F4, introduced in September 1988, is an even more sophisticated autofocus camera with the ability to track moving sub-

Mallard's ballet company. The "ballet company" was taken with a 400mm f/3.5 lens and a 1.4 teleconverter, giving an effective focal length of 560mm.

The three flying geese were taken from inside the car with a 300mm f/4.5 lens supported on the car window with a bean bag.

jects, predicting where the subject will be when the shutter opens. With Nikon improving its autofocus models, I expect that the other major manufacturers will do the same in time.

I have not rushed out to buy an autofocus camera. The primary use I can see for such capability with waterfowl would be for flying birds. But it is quite feasible to get good flying bird shots without autofocus by using the "follow focus" technique, especially with the faster-focusing lens systems. If you are planning to purchase a camera system with autofocus capability, be sure that it will also work easily in manual focus settings. The lenses should have comfortable, easy-to-use manual focusing rings. You might also inquire from a reputable repair shop about the failure rate of the particular model you are considering.

Focusing Screens

Most 35mm cameras come equipped with center-spot focusing screens, sometimes with a split-image feature as well. The center spot and split image are fine for focusing with lenses below 135mm in length. But a telephoto lens of 135mm or more cannot be focused as easily with these focusing screens. Unless there is a great deal of light, the center spot, especially the split-image spot, is likely to be half black and difficult to read.

A better choice for use with longer telephoto lenses is the overall-mat focusing screens, which enable you to see the whole field of view in focus. Often your subject will not be in the center of the photograph but off to one side for better composition. An overall-mat focusing screen aids in quick focusing no matter where in the field your subject may be. From the standpoint of composition, my preference is for a mat screen with faint crosshatch lines—five vertical and three horizontal lines. These lines help keep my horizons level and otherwise make composition easier. The proper focusing screen for use with telephoto lenses is well worth the modest investment.

Lenses—Large and Larger

The 180mm or 200mm 2.8 lens is versatile, compact, and readily hand held. Adding a 2x teleconverter gives the equivalent of a 360mm or 400mm f/5.6 lens. I tend to use this focal length lens more for scenic-type shots or for very close work with the tame waterfowl.

The 300mm lens in the f/4 range is also a good choice. It can be hand held. With relatively tame birds it is a fine lens for closeup shots. It also does

well for follow focusing or panning shots with flying birds. With a 1.4x teleconverter it becomes the equivalent of a 420mm f/5.6, or with a 2x teleconverter, 600mm f/8. With lenses of 300mm or more in length, the fast-focusing mechanisms make a considerable difference in ease of focusing on moving subjects (I use a 300mm lens more often than the 180mm for waterfowl photography).

The faster 300mm lenses are beautiful, but extremely expensive, pieces of equipment and probably justifiable only for professional wildlife photographers. The faster 300mm and 400mm lenses also require extra-sturdy tripods. With the addition of a 1.4x teleconverter, the 300mm f/2.8 lens becomes a 420mm f/5.6 lens. The flying mallard was taken with a 300mm f/2.8 lens and Fujichrome 100 film.

The 400mm f/5.6 lens should generally be supported on a tripod. Here again the faster-focusing mechanisms are definitely helpful. This lens weighs around 2.5 pounds (1.1 kilograms) and is a little over 10 inches (25.6 centimeters) long, so it can be carried quite a distance in a backpack. Using a 1.4x teleconverter with the 400mm f/5.6 lens gives the equivalent of a 560mm f/8 lens.

The 400mm f/3.5 lenses again require tripods or firm support, and a strong back to carry them. Their added speed makes them superb lenses for wildlife photography, but you'll have to mortgage the house to buy one.

In the 500mm range, Canon makes a very expensive f/4.5 version. Most companies, however, make only the mirror reflex type of lens in the 500mm range. The reflex lenses are of an entirely different type of construction, with much less glass in them than in the lenses previously discussed. The mirror reflex lenses are therefore lighter in weight, shorter in length, and more easily carried. They typically weigh less than two pounds (one kilogram). The big disadvantage of the reflex lens design is their fixed f-stop—f/8 in the case of a 500mm reflex lens. These lenses are also subject to producing little light rings from background light spots. Some people find these rings objectionable in their slides. The depth of field in a mirror reflex lens is also quite narrow.

The 600mm lens is a very heavy lens requiring a heavy-duty tripod for use. The 600mm f/4 lens weighs around 14 pounds (6.3 kilograms) in the Nikon version. The Canon 600mm f/4.5 weighs around 8.5 pounds (3.8 kilograms). A few of the professional wildlife photographers use these lenses, but many do not have one of that great a

Mallard flying in. The mallard flying straight towards me was taken with a 300mm f/2.8 lens. This is the most difficult kind of flying shot to set in focus.

length. The fast 300mm or 400mm with a 1.4 extender will certainly give acceptable quality photographs at much less cost than the 600mm lenses.

Zoom lenses are another possibility for wildlife photography. Their obvious advantage is a choice of a variety of focal lengths all in one lens, which makes composition easier. One lens can replace several that you might otherwise carry. On the negative side, zoom lenses are heavier and more cumbersome than the fixed-focal-length lenses and have higher f-stops for their size and weight. Zoom lenses also have the reputation of being a little less crisp and sharp than the equivalent fixed-focal-length lenses. Unless you already own a zoom telephoto, I would not recommend buying one to use for waterfowl or wildlife photography.

In summary, when choosing a lens for telephoto work, you must balance and weigh a number of considerations. Buy the lens that offers the most equitable combination of features you will want, consistent with your budget. If you plan to hand hold the lens or carry it any distance, stick with a lens in the 200mm f/2.8 or 300mm f/4.5 range. Then if you want greater focal length, you can add a teleconverter and a tripod with little extra weight or cost. The bigger, fancier lenses are fun to work with, but they are hard to justify in cost unless you sell a lot of photographs!

Motor Drives

Motor drives are not a necessity for wildlife or waterfowl photography, but they do add a dimension of flexibility, especially when shooting flying birds. The motor drive may enable you to fire off two or maybe even three shots of a bird taking off from water, for example. The nickel cadmium (nicad) battery pack gives a slight increase in speed over the standard battery pack for motor drives. The rechargeable nicad packs also function better than batteries in temperatures below freezing.

Tripods and Other Supports for Cameras with Telephoto Lenses

With telephoto lenses in the 300m length or longer, you will want to add a sturdy tripod to your equipment. Even though the lightweight 300mm lens can be hand held, there are times when you will need a tripod for it, such as when the ducks are very close to you. The closer your subject is to you, the greater the likelihood that minor camera movement will distort the picture. Also, a tripod or other support is useful as you wait for the right moment to snap the picture. Holding any size lens in place

for a long time is impractical.

The tripod should provide a firm support for your largest telephoto lens, camera, and motor drive at full height so you can use the camera from an upright standing position. Some tripods are wobbly when fully extended and, therefore, not useful for standing at full height. In addition to being fully functional for standing shots, the tripod should be equally firm for taking shots from a position very low to the ground. Often a "duck's-eye view" is more effective than "person's-eye view." Some tripods have removable center support posts and extra wide-spreading legs for work close to the ground. In general, heavier-weight tripods provide better support than light ones, being less subject to shaking from the wind or passing vehicles.

When buying a tripod, you must be sure to test the camera-and-lens combination you plan to use on it. Many standard tripod heads will not adequately support the weight of cameras with heavy lenses and a motor drive. The head should move easily in all directions so you can angle up for flying shots as well as down to the water, and smoothly follow focus on moving subjects. Black tripods will call less attention to your presence than silver metallic ones.

Car window mounts are useful to add to your equipment, especially for shooting in national wildlife refuges. Bushnell makes a simple window mount with a padded grip that fits over the glass. The mount is designed for use with telescopes, but works well with cameras without motor drives, or with motor-drive-equipped cameras if you reverse the handle to the outside of the window.

Bogen has recently introduced a window-mount camera support similar in design to the Bushnell telescope window mount, but designed for use with cameras. Bogen equipment should be readily available at local camera stores.

A much less expensive camera support for use on car windows, rocks, tree limbs, and so on is the beanbag type. A one-pound bag of small beans or rice makes an excellent support. Where weight is no problem, small lead shot makes a superior camera-support bag. My rice bag is encased in a camouflage bag.

Protecting Your Camera Equipment

Waterfowl photography is often done when the weather is harsh and cold. Winter may yield the best duck photographs in the middle and northern sections of the United States; however, cold weather extremes are hard on cameras and batteries. There are many tips that nature photographers have for survival in cold weather. Here are a few ideas that I have borrowed from others.

To protect camera batteries from extremes of cold, the camera body can be carried inside your parka or outer garment. A small hand-warmer can be taped to the back of the camera body to help heat the batteries when the camera must stay out in the cold for very long periods. Another use for tape in cold weather is to cover the exposed metal parts of the camera and tripod so your skin does not have to touch metal.

When bringing camera and lenses into a warm room or car after being outside in the cold, it is important to protect them from condensation. This is easily done by wrapping them in a large, airtight plastic bag until they completely warm up to room temperature. That way the condensation will fall on the plastic bag, not the camera and lenses.

Dust protection is also essential and a real problem when you are riding down dirt roads in search of an elusive quarry. Again, the large plastic garbage bag works well. You can have the camera ready to go, sitting on the car seat, if you completely encase it in an airtight plastic bag. Erwin and Peggy Bauer, wildlife photographers from Jackson, Wyoming, always ride with a camera ready for a chance shot by keeping it tucked in a plastic bag. Whenever I travel any distance with cameras, I cover the camera cases with a blanket or wrap them entirely in plastic bags to keep out dust.

Filters

People often ask if I have used colored filters for some of my bright sunset photographs. The answer is no. The only filter I use for waterfowl photography would be a polarizing filter with 180mm or smaller lenses. In most cases, adding a filter to a telephoto lens so greatly reduces the amount of light that you could not stop action with anything but the fastest films. Secondly, filters for the larger telephoto lenses are extremely expensive.

The shot of geese flying over the dock, in Chapter 2, was taken without a filter. Its warm, rosy color came from the late afternoon sun hitting fog. The color of sunset shots will seem more intense when you are shooting close to the sunset with a telephoto lens 300mm or larger because the field of view will encompass only the sky area of bright color. When we look at the whole scene without a camera lens, our eye sees the entire range of colors in the western sky—from brilliant ones near the sunset to the paler blues away from the sun. The scene we see with our naked eye may not seem nearly as colorful as what we selectively capture with the telephoto lens.

Film for Waterfowl Photography

Professional wildlife and waterfowl photographers use slide film, rather than print film, almost exclusively for their color work. Slide film has good color and the processing is less expensive than making prints for an entire roll of film. But most important of all, printing for books, magazines, calendars, and other publications is done from color separations made directly from slides.

Until recently, the film of choice has been Kodachrome 64 for wildlife, and Kodachrome 25 for stationary subjects. The two Kodachrome films had been preferred by publishers for their fine grain sharpness and their good color balance. Editors of nature publications are accustomed to the look of these two films. Until very recently, most of the images in the major nature publications taken with 35mm cameras were reproduced from Kodachrome 25 or 64 slides.

Now, however, a few editors of prominent nature publications are beginning to consider the use of Fujichrome 50 and occasionally Fujichrome 100. These editors also express interest in the newer Kodachrome 200 and the new Ektachrome 100 for wildlife photography. These faster films will certainly be a boon to photographers working with telephoto lenses. For a good discussion of recent editorial trends in films, see Boyd Norton's "Film Testing Update" in *The Guilfoyle Report* 6 (Fall 1987), pages 11 to 12.

Much of my earlier photography of waterfowl used Kodachrome 64 film. I like the colors and fine grain of the film and the clarity of the reproduction for both print enlargements and slide shows. Prints made from internegatives and prints made directly from the slide on Cibachrome processing are both sharp and clear in size 11 x 14. Cibachrome prints as large as 20 x 24 or 24 x 30 inches from Kodachrome slides remain sharp and clear. (I have not tried internegative prints in that size, so I cannot comment on those.)

For flying birds or closeup action shots with long telephoto lenses, however, Kodachrome 64 is just too slow. In order to stop action, one must shoot with a minimum speed of 1/500 second. With the 300mm f/4.5 lens, you must work with the lens nearly wide open, even in bright light, to use the correct f-stop, 5.6 at 1/500 second with Kodachrome 64. By adding one extra stop of light with film rated

The canvasback was taken on Ektachrome 100 film. Notice the deep blue of the water with Ektachrome films. (400mm f/3.5 lens)

ISO 100, action shots with the 300mm f/4.5 lens become more feasible, especially in low-light situations.

There are several brands of ISO 100 film on the market. I have used both the old Ektachrome 100 and Fujichrome 100. The old Ektachrome 100 does have more grain than the Kodachrome 64, but it has a deeper blue color for sky and water that I like. The color reproduction of the older Ektachrome 100 was not as vibrant as the Fujichrome 100, especially in the reds and yellows and greens.

In the spring of 1988, Kodak introduced its new Professional Ektachrome 100 Plus film, and in July 1988 its Ektachrome 100 HC in the amateur version. These new Ektachromes are reputed to compete favorably with the Fujichrome for color saturation. I will be interested to try them for waterfowl photography.

Fujichrome 50 and 100 have vibrant blues and greens, more lively colors than the blues and greens of Kodachrome. The old Fujichrome used to have a bit of yellow bias. Early in 1988, Fujichrome altered the film slightly in an attempt to remove that bias. The reds, oranges, and yellows in Fujichrome are especially brilliant. It is my under-standing that proper processing of Fujichrome slides is critical and that many laboratories may not do Fujichrome well. Many professional photographers are sending their Fujichrome slides to Kodak for ease of access and assurance of good quality processing.

The two photographs of the wood duck illustrate the subtle differences in color between Kodachrome 64 (top) and Fujichrome 100 (bottom). They were taken on the same day within one hour of each other.

An important note for users of Ektachrome and Fujichrome films: both of these films tend to leave a residue on the rollers and the film transport plate on the inside back of the camera. This residue can build up after two or three rolls of shooting, causing tiny thin horizontal streaks on the developed slides. To avoid these streaks when using either of these films, *gently* clean off the rollers and the film transport plate with lens paper or small cotton-tipped swabs dampened with pure rubbing alcohol. *Be careful to avoid touching the shutter curtain or shutter leaves in any way.* The shutter curtains should not be cleaned or brushed, as they are very delicate.

My early experimentation with Kodachrome 200

The shot of a swimming wood duck illustrates good color saturation with Kodachrome 64 film. (300mm f/2.8 lens)

This shot of the same wood duck was taken on Fujichrome 100 film within an hour of the previous shot above using the same lens. The Fujichrome colors are more lively and vibrant, particularly in the reds, yellows, and greens. (300mm f/2.8 lens)

The white tundra swans show up well against dark clouds.

was somewhat disappointing. Certainly the prospect of a fine-grain film with a 200 ASA is exciting to all wildlife photographers. But I was not pleased with the lack of crispness and definition in the K200. Also I found a shift in water color from blue to more green in the slide. However, for action shots under low-light conditions, the film is certainly worth considering.

Graininess is not always undesirable. Sometimes you want a soft effect to establish a particular mood in your photograph. Occasionally, I will choose an ISO 1000 film such as 3M's ISO 1000 for soft fog shots, to accentuate the misty, dreamy quality of the scene.

Finally, a comment on amounts of film I use and throw away! One of the questions I am frequently asked by other photographers is how many slides I keep from what I shoot. Nonphotographer spouses sometimes become quite concerned about the expense of photography when they see a wastebasket full of discarded slides. Film is not cheap, but considering the cost of your equipment and the cost of your valuable time, film is the least expensive component of the whole process of photography. With an interesting subject, I shoot many frames if it is something I might wish to print or publish. Sometimes I bracket exposures if I am not quite sure which will be the best. And often with moving subjects, I do not know if I have captured on film the positions that are most pleasing. Frequently I keep only a half dozen or so from each roll of thirty-six slides, especially when I photograph flying birds!

Beyond the Camera—Outfitting the Photographer

In addition to properly selected camera gear, successful waterfowl photography requires some attention to properly outfitting the photographer. Creativity flourishes in comfort. If you are too cold, too wet, or too cramped in an uncomfortable position with binding clothes, you are much less likely to take good photographs.

Clothing for photography should be functional, loose fitting for ease of movement, and preferably of a color that will blend into the background. Neutral colors like tan, green, brown, or gray will blend in better than bright colors. Hunters' camouflage or surplus Army camos make good photography clothes for wildlife shooting.

If you plan to shoot in damp, marshy areas, waterproof footwear or maybe even chest waders are helpful. I can sit or kneel in damp reeds at the river's edge wearing chest waders and be warm and dry for several hours. The colder the weather, the greater the necessity for warm, waterproof boots and clothing.

In late fall and winter, remember that you will be spending a lot of time sitting still while out photographing the ducks and geese. Keeping hands and feet warm seems to be the biggest problem. Leather gloves work better than mittens, of course, for operating the shutter and focusing rings. In really cold weather, my Sorel boots lined with felt padding keep my feet warm while I stand or sit waiting for the birds. I use these boots with an inner polypropylene sock and an outer wool sock. For a good discussion of wearing apparel and tips on camera equipment aids for cold weather, see the article by Jeff Foott in *Outdoor Photographer*, February 1988, pages 44 to 46.

One additional piece of equipment that I always carry is a kneeling pad. It saves both my knees and my clothing from wear and tear since I spend a lot of time on my knees when I photograph waterfowl. A gardener's foam kneeling pad or a camouflage pillow work well. Either can double as a sitting pad. Once in a while, I use a full-length foam pad for stretching out flat on the ground at water's edge. This is especially useful in the winter on snow and ice!

Geese Landing in Fog. This illustrates the kind of soft romantic mood that can be obtained on bright foggy days.

4 / Blinds and Camouflage

Lacking a tame population of wild birds, the photographer must adapt techniques of the hunter for closeup shots of single birds or small groups of birds. This chapter outlines various types of blinds ("hides" to the British) suitable for photography. A reference list at the end of the chapter gives names of companies and their addresses for purchasing blinds and materials for making your own blind.

Make Yourself Disappear

There are several ways the photographer can disappear into the surroundings without an elaborate blind. First and foremost, no matter what clothing you are wearing, you should remember that it is movement that catches the attention of both waterfowl and animals. If you sit perfectly still for a long time, wildlife probably will not notice you, particularly if you are partially screened behind grasses or bushes. Being still and making very slow movements at all times will aid in getting closer photographs of birds and animals.

Wearing clothing the color of the background also helps one disappear. Hunting stores have a wide variety of camouflage clothing and gear. Be sure to buy clothing that is quiet when you move or walk. A black tripod will show up less than a bright metallic one. And black lenses are less obvious than white ones. Owners of white-colored lenses sometimes put camouflage tape on their lens hoods when photographing wildlife.

A simple aid to disappearing into bushes or reeds is the packaged camouflage netting available in two sizes from hunting stores. The netting fits easily into a jacket pocket or backpack. It can be draped around bushes and over your lens and yourself when you are seated in the field. Camouflage clothing plus a length of this portable netting makes an inexpensive way to hide yourself from view.

Inexpensive Homemade Blinds

A friend of mine has been taking wonderful photographs of both small birds and waterfowl using a blind made from a stepladder covered with an old bedspread. Almost any type of covering will work for a blind, but I do not recommend burlap, because it sheds pieces of thread onto you and your camera gear. The material should be securely fastened to whatever supports it so nothing will flap in the wind. Secondly, it is helpful if you can pick up your blind to slowly move it into a better position while you are hidden inside.

Some people have constructed blinds for waterfowl photography out of chicken wire covered with dark material, finishing up the blind with reeds, grasses, or small bushes to make it blend better with its environment. In constructing a blind, be sure you allow sufficient room for yourself, camera, and tripod to sit comfortably for several hours at a time. You must screen yourself from view not only from the sides but also from the top so flying birds will not spot you.

Several types of camouflage material are available by the yard from hunting supply shops. The materials range from very thin mesh material suitable for view ports to heavier opaque materials suitable for sides of blinds. With opaque materials, you do not need to worry about movement inside the blind being seen. Velcro fastening or zippers along the slit for your lens are very helpful. You will want a long opening so that you can adjust the height of your lens from ground level to top of grass and bush level. (See listings at the end of this chapter for supplies of camouflage materials by the yard.)

John Shaw, in his fine book *The Nature Photographer's Complete Guide to Professional Field Techniques*, gives directions for making a projection stand into a simple portable photo blind. With a little sewing ability, John's blind can be made relatively inexpensively. Here, reprinted with permission from AMPHOTO BOOKS, are the directions for making John's blind.

The traditional blind is constructed of four uprights with a cloth covering, supported with guy ropes running from each corner. From my field experience I know this is not a good design for several reasons:

You need a design that allows you to shoot at infinitely variable heights. *Working on a ground nesting bird demands a different shooting level than working in the middle of cattails where you must photograph over the vegetation. Ideally, one blind should cover the whole range.*

The blind must be compact when folded, easily portable, and quick to erect at the site. *Running guy ropes is not a fast job.*

It must remain vertical even when erected on uneven terrain. *This is one of the main failings of the designs for the blinds you see in most books. They must be set up on absolutely flat ground since they offer no provision for adjusting leg lengths. How can you work on the side of a hill?*

The blind should be self-supporting. *No matter how carefully you choose a location, with a guyed blind you usually end up about two feet in the wrong direction. With a self-supporting blind you just pick it up and move it wherever you want it.*

The best blind frame that I know of can be purchased ready-made: it is a standard Welt Safe-Lock projection stand. It is self-supporting, with individually adjustable legs that screw into a flat top piece. Folded up, the legs attach to the top and there is even a handle to carry it all. When you add a covering the blind takes roughly three minutes to erect.

You need to add a leg section to make it go to stand-up height. Buy four 3-foot lengths of ⅞-inch diameter tubing. Drill a ¼-inch hole through the tubing about 6 inches from either end. Now pull the crutch tips from the stand's legs and drill another ¼-inch hole 3 inches in from the end of each leg. Slip the tubing into the legs, line up the holes, and drop a ¼-inch bolt through the hole (or be fancy and buy a thumbscrew and wingnut for 30 cents per leg). Use the lower hole and the tubing will be sticking out about 3 inches. Use the top hole and it will be out 2½ feet. Of course you can still use each leg's locking collar to adjust the length. On my blind the legs go from a

minimum length of 3 feet to a maximum of 7 feet.

For covering the blind buy any material that is strong, cheap, and dull colored so you won't be interrupted by a stream of curiosity-seekers. Measure your projection stand and sew a cover to fit. Make it just long enough for the regular legs, without the extensions you've added. Most of the time you won't be using the blind that tall and the extra material will be in the way. You can always add a skirt to the bottom, attaching it with Velcro strips.

For the lens, cut a hole and attach a sleeve about 12 inches in diameter and 12 inches long. This allows you to track from side to side without the lens pushing against the blind itself. Put a small peep hole in every side. Make a door by leaving a back seam open. To keep the door tightly closed run Velcro down its length (Velcro is much better than zippers or blanket pins since it cannot jam or get lost). Add a few pockets to the inside to hold odd items, or even rocks if you need to weight the cover down.

One overlooked item is what you sit on in a blind. Camp stools and folding chairs do not work well except on hard, level ground. Use a camp stool on soft or wet dirt and soon you're below the camera level. The best seats I've found are the five-gallon plastic pails used to package joint compound or institutional foods. You can usually find one among a restaurant's refuse.

If you're working on a very windy area, set a big rock on the top platform to stabilize the blind. Once inside, you can move your location if you have to. Pick up the tripod with one hand, the blind with the other, and tip-toe into position. I know it sounds rather silly, but it works.

Ready-Made Blinds for Photography

For those who prefer to purchase a ready-made blind, there are two slightly different designs available for under $200 by mail order, one from Leonard Rue Enterprises, the other one from Lepp and Associates. Both use a lightweight supporting tent-style frame with a fitted cover. The Leonard Rue Enterprises version offers 6 screened viewing windows on 5 sides, a main photographic snout and 4 additional smaller camera ports so photos can be taken from 5 sides of the blind. The Lepp and Associates version is made from camouflage material, with windows that may be fully open or covered with see-through camouflage screening attached with Velcro fasteners. Both models are self-supporting, but come with pegs and tie-downs for use on windy days. The addresses for catalogues from these two organizations appear at the end of this chapter.

John Shaw's photograph illustrates one version of the floating "muskrat-house" blind.

Floating Muskrat-House Blind

For the adventuresome photographer, the floating muskrat-house blind enables one to get right out onto the water with the waterfowl. These blinds are useful in small bodies of water where waterfowl are concentrated near good access for the blind. The photograph by John Shaw illustrates one version of the floating blind.

Glenn D. Chambers, corporate photographer for Ducks Unlimited, has written a comprehensive article on the construction and use of the muskrat-house floating photography blind. Here is his article, reprinted with permission of *Ducks Unlimited Magazine.*

MAKIN' LIKE A MUSKRAT

George Shira III, often known as the father of wildlife photography, was the first to photograph wild creatures from a camouflaged, floating canoe. That was back in the 1890s. Since then contrivances for sneaking up on wild birds have become more sophisticated and specialized.

Many photographers, today use an innovative replica of a muskrat house for photographing waterfowl. It's an ingenious idea, for it takes an object ducks and geese often see in the marsh and tailors it to conceal a photographer and his gear. At the same time, this hide is mobile enough to allow ease in navigating through the marsh. A practiced user can get within incredibly close range of his unsuspecting subjects.

I call the use of this contraption the art of tubing, because most devices of this nature are kept afloat with a large inflatable inner tube. Make-believe muskrat homes come in all sizes and are camouflaged with everything from cattails to phragmites, three-square, bulrushes and willows.

Let's examine the anatomy of one of these marsh masterpieces. The first and most basic component is a 24 x 12.00 rubber inner tube. On top of this lies a donut-shaped platform which is lashed to the tube and constructed of 1/2-inch exterior plywood with an outside diameter of 40 inches and an inside diameter of 24 inches. The dome above the platform is created using three pieces of 1/2-inch aluminum conduit tubing 84 inches long. These are bent into three arches and anchored to the platform from the bottom using 1/4-inch bolts.

The basic covering over the conduit framework is burlap or canvas. Canvas makes a better cover than burlap because it is more opaque. The loose weave of burlap sometimes permits enough light to filter through to expose the movement of the photographer inside, even when vegetative camouflage is thatched to the exterior. If burlap is used, at least two layers are needed. I also cover the burlap or canvas with fish netting to facilitate attaching the natural camouflage. Camouflage the floater using whatever vegetation is predominant in the marsh where you will be photographing. Cattails are a natural for this purpose because they are easy to thatch and are found in most marshes.

Entry/exit openings can be made using hinged doors or roll-up/roll-down doorways. I have one model that has no door at all: I just lift it over my head and shoulders like a huge helmet.

I have some special features in my muskrat houses that I've developed through the years. I use two-inch Fastex quick release nylon buckles (available at wilderness outfitters) and a nylon saddle that snaps into these buckles after I'm situated inside. The ends of the nylon buckles are attached to the innermost circle of the platform. Or you can simply cut a seat out of plywood and lash it to the inner tube with nylon rope. If you use this method, you should carry a knife so that you can cut the rope in an emergency. The saddle helps prevent cold soakings when tubing in marshes with uneven bottom depths where you might unexpectedly take a step into water over your waders. The saddle can be quickly unsnapped in an emergency or when tubing in shallow water. I have also designed a low, triangular-shaped camera stand that is mounted to the platform. It works like a tripod permitting me to lock my camera to a fluid head mount so that I don't have to fight camera movement created by waves or "off-hand" shooting. It also permits free hand movement while pushing the blind over water from one area of the

marsh to another. Windows strategically located for additional viewing are also helpful.

The platform inside the house is equipped with a 3/4-inch high plywood retaining ledge or lip surrounding the 24-inch hole to help prevent equipment from rolling off into the water. Indoor-outdoor carpeting is useful in preventing excessive wear and tear on equipment and for reducing the interior noise level. It is surprising how much racket can be created by laying a canister of film on a wooden platform where the sound is amplified over a huge hollow tube resting on water! Thermoses, lunches and gadget bags can be stowed around the sides and to the rear of the platform. The cost of materials for a muskrat house will run about $100.

Some tubing precautions are noteworthy. Entering or exiting the blind are the most dangerous times for the photographer and his or her equipment. Plan your tubing expedition so you have an easy place for accomplishing these operations. Ice poses a problem too. It's difficult to maneuver the tube through even thin ice. The noise and confusion this creates frightens wildlife, and presents the perils of punctures, which can leave you carrying your own house back to the car.

Know the marsh where you will be tubing. Explore your proposed navigation route in advance to become familiar with water depth and underwater obstacles. The ideal water depth for tubing is waist deep for it allows the photographer the choice of shooting while standing up or sitting down in the saddle. The opportunity to take a rest in the saddle from time to time is important because tubing is a strenuous activity. It is difficult to tube in water that is less than knee deep because in this situation, most of your body is above water and thus crammed into the small interior of the house. Tubing is not for those who have claustrophobic tendencies.

When tubing, move slowly. Most marsh animals including waterfowl can be approached if you take it easy. Observe as you go for some neat photographic experiences can show up unexpectedly. With continued tubing in the same area, some ducks will get wise to your little pile of moving cattails. For this reason, the first few attempts you make could well be the most productive. However, during migration when new birds are arriving daily, tubing may improve as the season progresses. It is a lot like hunting. Wind conditions, sunlight and temperature can all affect the behavior of your subjects. So I go tubing every possible day in hopes of hitting a good day when the birds are working well. Tubing outside the hunting season has been the most profitable for me. The birds tend to be less spooky during the winter and spring. And don't forget, spring is the time when the birds are sporting those bright breeding plumages that are extremely photogenic.

If you're the kind of person that likes company, don't worry about "living alone" in your marsh home. While tubing in the Ponass wetlands of Saskatchewan I had one persistent muskrat that visited me daily—inside my house. That was a distressing experience for those sharp teeth could have played havoc with my chest waders or inner tube—two pieces of equipment I didn't want punctured. Snakes are also attracted to the shelter of this floating home. Though you can usually see them approaching for quite some distance, I defy you to get their attention before they are inside with you, eyeball to eyeball. While tubing for wood ducks in flooded pin oak stands along the Mississippi River I've had large carp brush against my legs. Unfortunately, hand fishing was illegal! And once, on a cold spring morning in a northern Manitoba marsh, I tipped up the muskrat house to get inside only to find at least a thousand leeches attached to the underside of the tube.

The epitome of muskrat floaters is yet to come. I'm working on a design that has a hinged top which will permit safer and more comfortable entry and exit. Once perfected, I'll share it will you.

Suppliers of Camouflage Materials

Cabela's
812 13th Avenue
Sidney, Nebraska 69160

Sprocor, Inc.
Route 2, Box 402
Queenstown, Maryland 21658

Suppliers of Ready-made Blinds

Leonard Rue Enterprises
138 Millbrook Road
Blairstown, New Jersey 07825

Lepp and Associates
P.O. Box 6240
Los Osos, California 93412

Canada geese at sunrise on a misty, fog shrouded pond on one of those magical mornings in the fall.

5 / Notes on Composition

This chapter discusses some of the basic elements of composition and suggests points to consider in planning and shooting your waterfowl scenes and close-ups. Planning ahead and being aware of composition before you press the shutter will help ensure more artistic and pleasing shots.

Point of View—Intended Communication

A photograph that is intended to be more than a record or snapshot should communicate something to the viewer. To create an effective photograph, the photographer should have in mind what it is he or she wishes to convey. Deciding why you wish to shoot a particular scene or bird helps in making the many decisions about how to take the photograph. You might, for example, wish to portray the peace and tranquility of waterfowl at rest. Or you might wish to show the dramatic action of ducks as they explode off the water into flight when alarmed. In both these examples, before one can make decisions about choice of lenses, film, position of the photographer, time of day to take the photograph, desired lighting, composition, and so on, the intended communication needs to be clear.

Among the kinds of questions you might ask along these lines are the following:

- What feeling or emotion do I wish to evoke?
- Do I want to portray fright, conflict, anger?
- Do I wish to show motion, action?
- Do I want the viewer to be directly involved with the subject or to be a distant observer?
- Do I want the viewer to be amused?
- Do I wish to show peace and harmony? or the nobility and majesty of the birds?

The answers to these kinds of questions enable you to make decisions about which lenses and film to use, where to place yourself relative to the birds and the light source, what time of day to try to take the photograph, what kind of weather would be desirable, where to place the subject in the frame, and so on.

Active Versus Static Composition

If the photographer wishes to suggest to the viewer a feeling of peace, harmony, and tranquility, a number of elements besides the obvious one of picturing birds at rest can be used to support the concept. Soft, diffuse lighting appears more tranquil than strong lighting and dark shadows. Cool colors such as blues, greens, and lavender are more restful than vivid colors like yellow and red. Muted tones are more restful than bold, clear colors.

But for supporting the message of peace and harmony, the most important element in a composition is the direction of the lines in the photograph. Horizontal lines suggest rest and tranquility. Upright lines suggest growth, movement, action. Diagonal lines suggest action, movement, conflict, and discord. Therefore, if you wish to convey a feeling of rest, use a horizontal camera frame and predominantly horizontal lines in the composition.

The horizontals may come from the distant horizon, a line of treetops, a movement in the water, or the birds themselves. In addition to the lines that you actually see in the picture, there may also be implied lines, as in the case of flying or swimming birds. Here the implied line moves horizontally in the direction of the bird's movement. A duck flying from left to right parallel to the water or ground implies a horizontal line in the direction of flight. A landing bird implies a line down or diagonally in the direction of the descent.

Twilight landing. This illustrates both actual and implied horizontal lines, enhancing the peaceful tranquility of the scene. (300mm f/4.5 lens)

The photograph titled "Twilight Landing" illustrates both actual and implied horizontal lines. There are horizontal lines in the horizon, in the fog bank, and in the movement of the water, as well as in the overall pattern of the geese themselves. There are implied lines of motion from left to right along the flight path. The peaceful tranquility of the scene is further enhanced by the soft quality of the fog and the muted tones of the late afternoon sunlight. (For further discussion of light and fog, see Chapter 7.)

It is important not to forget the implied lines of movement in your composition. If you ignore them, the photograph may appear unbalanced. Leave room in the picture for birds or animals in motion to fly or swim into the picture. Otherwise the implied line of motion will carry the eye outside of the frame.

Another implied line comes from the direction of gaze of an animal or person. In close-ups of waterfowl, I almost always focus on the eye of my subject, something autofocus cameras won't do, by the way. The eye is the natural focal point for a closeup animal or bird shot. If the eye is in focus, the rest of the bird need not be as sharp. If your subject is to one side of the frame, usually it should be look-

ing into the picture rather than outside of it from the short side. Our eyes will follow the direction of its gaze, so there should be room for the bird to look as well as room to move in the frame for the picture to look balanced. When the animal or bird is looking directly at the photographer or viewer, there is greater flexibility for placing it within the frame.

We have seen in the photograph "Twilight Landing" how horizontal lines support the concept of rest and harmony. What about upright or vertical lines? Vertical lines are less restful, more active, more alive. If your intention is to convey movement, life, or activity you might consider using an upright frame and vertical lines for your composition. In the example of the blue-winged teal, not only does the subject fit better into an upright frame, but the vertical and diagonal lines of the bird add to the idea of motion as he preens himself.

Still more alive and active than the vertical line is the diagonal line. Diagonals imply strong movement, action, force, conflict, or strong emotion. Straight diagonals are stronger than curving diagonals. In the example of the bathing hooded merganser, the obvious action of the duck is supported by the flying water drops. Motion is further emphasized by the diagonal lines from bill to top of the head and in his crest feathers. The bird looks very

much alive and moving as he shakes off the water.

The upright composition with vertical and diagonal lines adds to the idea of motion and life as the blue-winged teal preens himself. (300mm f/4.5 lens)

Hooded merganser bathing. In this example, the very obvious action of the duck is supported by the flying water drops. Motion is further emphasized by the strong diagonal lines from bill to top of the head and in his crest feathers. (400mm f/3.5 lens)

Placement of the Subject in the Frame

When composing the photograph through the lens, where should the main subject be placed? Depending on what you wish to communicate about the subject, you may want it to be very close and prominent in the foreground, or you may want it to be smaller, showing more of its environment and surroundings. Most people recognize that putting the main subject or focal point in the center of the picture usually does not produce a balanced composition. But if not in the center, then where? An easy guide to use in planning your composition is the rule of thirds. Imagine the frame divided into equal thirds from side to side and from top to bottom by two horizontal and two vertical lines. Place your subjects somewhere outside of the middle block, at or near the intersection of two of the lines. That way your subject will be far enough from the edge, but not in the center. If you wish to emphasize the foreground, place your subject at the top left intersection, leaving the bottom ⅔ of the frame for foreground. If, on the other hand, you wish to emphasize the bird in its environment, place him in the bottom right or left intersection.

Placement of the subject in the lower right third of the picture can be tricky. Unless there is something on the left of the composition for balance, it is usually better to avoid putting the subject in the lower right corner. For example, birds shown against plain water or plain sky (negative space opposite the subjects) should be placed anywhere but the lower right corner. There is a psychological weighting of the lower right corner, which makes it appear heavier than the top and lower left corners. If you place your subject in the lower right corner with nothing to balance it on the left and top, the picture will appear to be sinking to the right corner. Reverse the placement, putting the subject in the lower left corner and leaving the negative space in the lower right, and the composition appears balanced.

Because of the phenomenon of the weighted lower right corner, it is often better with flying birds in a plain sky to have them flying from left to right, leaving negative space on the lower right. Remember that you can turn over a slide and print it in reverse! "Twilight Landing" is printed in reverse because it looked better that way.

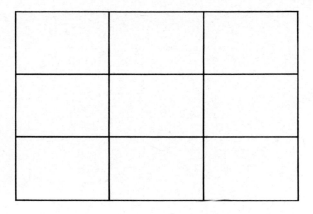

Canada geese feeding. Placing the subject in the lower third of the photograph emphasizes the birds in their environment. (180mm f/2.8 lens)

Canada swimming. Placing the subject in the lower right corner with nothing to balance it on the top and left gives the appearance the picture is sinking on the right corner.

Canada swimming. Reverse the same composition by flopping the slide over, leaving the negative space in the lower right corner, and the composition appears balanced. We perceive the lower right corner to have more weight than the lower left corner.

Black duck/ice. With close views of one or two birds, following the rule of thirds often makes a more pleasing composition than one that places the bird in the middle of the frame. (400mm f/3.5 lens)

The odd couple—mallard and woody. Extremely closeup views of ducks and geese are more effective when taken from a duck's-eye view at ground or water level. The impact of the interaction between Sir Francis Wood Drake and Lady Mallard would have been lost had this shot been taken from a standing position, looking down on the ducks.

Mallard duckling. In this photo taken with a 180mm f/2.8 lens, the out-of-focus background highlights the individual feathers and fuzz on the duckling's back.

With moderately close views of one or two birds, generally the subject and focal point should follow the rule of thirds to one side up or down from the middle. The duck pictured would be less pleasing if he were centered in the composition. Here he has room to move into the frame and the negative space is in the weighted lower right corner.

With extreme close-ups where the bird fairly well fills the frame, placing it in the center may be the most pleasing arrangement. For example, the shot of "Windy Woody" on page 4 and the flying mallard on page 29 are good examples of subjects that need to be centered in the frame.

Extreme closeup shots have the most impact, more directly involving the viewer with the bird than shots taken from a distance, where the bird is smaller in the frame. When you want the viewer to be directly engaged with the bird, take a straight-on shot from the duck's-eye-view-level. Ground- or water-level close-ups are much more effective than those taken from a standing position looking down on the duck. The impact of the interaction between Sir Francis Wood Drake and Lady Mallard would be lost if this shot had been taken from a standing height above the birds.

Depth and Perspective

A photograph, like a painting, is a flat surface that we perceive to have depth or perspective if certain elements are present in the picture to support that perception. Perspective is defined by the *American Heritage Dictionary of the English Language* as "any of various techniques for representing three-dimensional objects and depth relationships on a two-dimensional surface."

Some of the more natural pictorial elements that suggest distance and depth are the following:

1. converging lines of things we know are parallel, such as paths, roads, railroads, brooks, plowed fields;
2. diminishing size of objects we know to be similar in size, such as telephone poles, electric-line towers, trees, flowers, grasses, reeds;
3. receding lines of objects that we know to be square or rectangular, such as building lines;

We can also create the perception of depth by

4. placing one object behind another object;
5. softening the atmosphere in the background; and
6. modeling an object through directional

lighting, which casts shadows (flat lighting without shadows tends to flatten the appearance of the object).

When photographing a single animal or bird, we want it to appear as though it has substance—weight and form. If the duck's body is rounded, we want it to look rounded. Similarly, when photographing a scene, we want it to appear to have depth and space. The inclusion of one or more of the elements above will enhance the viewer's perception of depth in the photograph.

Depth of Field and Perspective

The photographer has readily at hand one additional means of suggesting perspective to the viewer, and that is through control of the depth of field of the camera lens. In photographic terms, depth of field refers to that space in front of and behind the subject where the focus is still sharp. With long telephoto lenses and close-in subjects, the depth of field will be very shallow. For a 300mm lens at f/4.5, focused on a subject 10 feet (3 meters) away, the depth of field is from 9.8 feet to 10.2 feet, or .4 feet (12 centimeters). Move the subject 20 feet away (6 meters), and the depth of field increases, becoming from 19.4 to 20.7 feet, or 1.3 feet (40 centimeters) (*Nikon Handbook*). In other words, the closer the subject of focus, the narrower the depth of field at a given f-stop. (With a higher f-stop, the depth of field increases for a given distance.)

What does depth of field have to do with perspective in the photograph? We perceive a sharply focused subject seen against an out-of-focus background to have depth and form. The in-focus subject will seem some distance away from the blurred background. Sometimes it is useful to choose a lower f-stop so that the background will be blurred and out of focus. This technique makes your subject stand out from the background, giving it the form and substance it might not have when shown against an in-focus background. Blurring the background also prevents it from competing for attention with the main subject. It is important to think about depth of field and use it to support the message you wish to get across in your photograph.

In the photograph of the baby mallard ducking, the background is blurred out of focus. Had the background been sharply focused, the impact of the duckling would have been diminished. With an out-of-focus background, one sees the texture of individual feathers and fuzz in the duckling's back.

The hooded merganser was snapped near the end of a lengthy courtship routine as he reared up in the water crowing an invitation to his lady. (400mm f/3.5 lens)

Diving ducks make interesting subjects to photograph. This canvasback duck has just broken to the surface of the water as he came up from his dive for corn. (400mm f/3.5 lens)

6 / Adding Interest to Compositions

Unusual Behavior

To create a photograph beyond the ordinary, the photographer must plan ahead. If it is action you wish to capture on film, you must know how and where you are likely to find waterfowl engaged in some activity other than their usual lazy swimming or sleeping. Courtship behaviors, bathing and preening, wing stretching, diving for food, taking flight, or landing on the water all offer interesting and challenging possibilities for the photographer. Springtime courtship routines are great fun to watch, especially those of hooded mergansers, ruddy ducks, and Western grebes. Tundra swans also have elaborate dances that they perform on occasion. The hooded merganser was photographed at the very end of his lengthy courtship display as he reared back in the water, crowing an invitation to his lady.

Bathing and preening often takes place after ducks have eaten. Feed them a little corn or bread to bring them in close, then sit quietly and watch for bathers. Diving ducks can be photographed on their way down for food or as they come up from their dive. Be prepared to waste lots of film when trying to photograph divers! The canvasback pictured had just broken to the surface of the water as he came up from his dive for corn. The splash of water as well as the water drops on his back help make this a more unusual photograph. For this kind of close-up, a shutter speed of 1/1000 second is necessary to stop action.

Flying Birds

Flying birds are much more of a challenge to photograph than sitting or swimming birds. Getting good shots in focus with wings in a pleasing position takes a fair degree of practice and skill. While a motor drive is not essential for flying bird shots, it can be helpful. A motor drive also adds weight that helps to balance the camera when you are using heavy telephoto lenses. For the maximum speed with successive shots, use nickel cadmium rechargeable batteries in your battery pack rather than the standard AA batteries. With the Nikon F3 motor drive, the nicad battery pack fires at 5.5 frames per second, compared to 4 frames per second with a standard battery pack.

Flight shots can be taken either with a hand-held camera and a lightweight telephoto lens or with longer lenses and a camera mounted on a tripod. When you use a tripod, all the fittings must be sufficiently loose to easily move the camera up, down, and sideways. For flying bird shots, some people prefer a fluid-ball tripod head that moves in all directions. The ball head must be sturdy enough to support a camera with a heavy telephoto lens attached.

One method for photographing flying birds is to preset a point of focus on the lens, follow the bird until it reaches that point, and then press the shutter. I use another technique for my flying bird shots, that of "follow focusing." With the bird farther away than I wish to shoot, I begin focusing on him, changing the focus as he flies in closer. With my motor drive set on continuous frames, I press the shutter when I think the bird is in focus and close enough for a good shot. The fast internal focusing lenses are of great help in this situation.

Flying bird shots are somewhat easier when the subjects are flying a course parallel to you. You can follow their approach with one fluid motion of the camera, snapping them as they pass in front of you.

When the birds are flying directly towards you, the focusing is more difficult. The closer the bird to

Snow goose clowns. Flying shots are easiest when the birds are flying a course parallel to you rather than oncoming towards you. You can follow their approach with one fluid motion of the camera, snapping the shot as they pass in front of you. These snow geese were taken with a 300mm f/4.5 lens on a tripod.

you, the faster he moves out of focus due to the diminishing depth of field with closer objects. The flying-in mallard on page 29 was taken with a 300mm lens follow focusing on the bird as he flew towards me. I was very fortunate that of the three shots fired, two were in focus.

One might think that the flying bird situation would be ideal for an autofocus camera since 300mm lenses for autofocus cameras are available at this time. But with the exception of the Nikon F-4 and the Minolta 7000i, the present autofocus technology is not adequate to capture flying birds at close range. For one thing, the autofocusing spot is a very small one directly in the center of the frame. That spot must be constantly on the subject of focus. More importantly, the automatic focus mechanisms of most autofocus cameras cannot change quickly enough to keep flying birds in focus as they approach. The closer your subject is to you, the faster it moves out of focus. At the time of this writing, only the Nikon F4 and the Minolta 7000i have the capability of following a moving subject and predicting where it will be when the shutter opens.

Flying bird shots may be made somewhat more interesting by the inclusion of foreground or background elements in the scene. For example, cloud patterns or dramatic sky behind the birds may add to the composition. Clouds in the background considerably change the exposure needed, so be sure to remember to open up as much as a whole stop or a stop and ⅓ when shooting against white-clouded sky.

Foreground elements like branches, treetops, reeds, grasses, and the like also may enhance a composition. Unless the birds are very close to the branches or grasses, however, they will appear out of focus when you are shooting with a telephoto lens. The shot of geese descending over the treetops was taken just as the birds reached the tree line. The tree branches balance the five incoming birds and add interest to the composition.

Swimming Birds

A duck or goose swimming all by itself with nothing but water in the background is probably not the most interesting photograph. Adding elements such as branches, grasses, reeds, or leaves to the background or foreground may greatly improve the shot. For these elements to be in focus, the

Foreground elements like three branches add interest to compositions with flying birds. The Canada geese had to be very close to the branches for both birds and branches to be in focus with a telephoto lens. (180mm f/2.8 lens)

geese must be swimming in close proximity to them. The geese pictured illustrate the use of background grasses in a shot that includes some of the environment as well as the birds. The photograph of the geese with grass was taken with a 180mm lens at a distance of 25 to 30 feet (7.5 to 9 meters). They were swimming close enough to the grasses that both geese and the grass could be in focus.

Another approach is to shoot through foreground branches, weeds, or grass to the birds behind. Focusing through foreground material adds depth to the scene because the foreground is obviously in front of the birds. In this situation, focus on the birds and hope the foreground will be in sufficient focus. Remember that the foreground color will affect your exposure. Even though you may be looking at dark colors behind the foreground, the camera meter will see the lighter foreground. Dry grasses, for example, are very light in color, so you may need to open up ⅓ to ⅔ of a stop for correct exposure of the darker colors behind the grasses.

Nesting Waterfowl and Young Birds

When photographing nesting birds, take great

care to avoid disturbing the sitting mother. Like most wild creatures, ducks and geese have very little tolerance for intrusion into their space when nesting or guarding their young. Eggs left unguarded may be snatched up by hawks, snakes, raccoons, or other predators.

A floating "muskrat-house" blind is ideal for photographing nesting waterfowl. But equally fine photographs can be obtained from land at places where the birds are accustomed to being close to people. Parks and golf-course ponds and certain well-visited national wildlife refuges offer good possibilities for finding nests or young that can be approached close enough for good photographs.

The western grebe pictured was photographed from a portable blind set up beside a busy roadway at a North Dakota national wildlife refuge. Because these birds were accustomed to people and activity near their nesting sites, it was possible to get good shots from the blind 25 to 30 feet (7.5 to 9 meters) away from their nests without disturbing them.

Young ducklings and goslings are best photographed in parks or at golf courses where their parents are used to being fed by people. The young birds learn very quickly where they can get han-

The photograph of the Canada geese with grasses illustrates use of background elements in focus to add information to an environmental portrait. (180mm f/2.8 lens)

This nesting Western grebe was photographed from a portable canvas blind set up at the edge of a national wildlife refuge lake in North Dakota's prairie pothole region.

Shooting through branches of grasses to the Canada geese beyond adds depth to the scene. (300mm f/4.5 lens)

douts. I have watched ducklings and goslings swimming around, ignoring whatever adults might be present. But the minute a small child appears on the scene, the young birds swim straight toward the child, expecting to be fed.

Ducklings and goslings can be enticed with tiny bits of whole-grain breads. They do not handle corn kernels well unless it is cracked corn. Whole corn is good for adult ducks and geese.

Simplify, Unify, and Isolate

Photographers often include too much in their pictures. Some of the most pleasing and effective compositions are the most simple ones. Too many birds or cluttered backgrounds and foregrounds can detract from the impact of the photograph. The simpler and plainer the background, the more the subject commands attention.

One way to simplify the background is to photograph the birds against open water. Using a fast shutter speed gives sharp lines to any waves or ripples in the water. A slower shutter speed, like 1/60 second, smooths out the water to a pleasing pattern of lights and darks without sharp edges. The subject must be sitting still, of course, for you to use a slow shutter speed. In the photograph of the green-winged teal, the water behind the duck echoes his colors but does not detract from him because of its soft edges.

Snow and ice make good simplified backgrounds for both closeup and scenic shots. Snow can turn an ugly muddy riverbank into a delightful setting for waterfowl. Besides covering unsightly details, the snow covering provides a unity of color that simplifies the photograph. White backgrounds also offer good contrast for dark-colored geese and ducks. The black duck, for example, looks dull when photographed against muddy banks or water. But isolating a black duck on snow or ice is something else entirely.

A slow shutter speed like 1/30 or 1/60 second smoothes the water to a pleasing pattern without sharp edges. The water behind the green-winged teal echoes his colors but does not detract from him because of its soft blended edges. (300mm f/4.5 lens)

The black duck isolated against snow or ice makes an effective portrait shot. He would be much less visible against a dark background of water or riverbank. (400mm f/3.5 lens)

The head of this wood duck is well focused with bright color, but the mixed background detracts from the overall effect.

The simpler background of this wood duck portrait makes a more pleasing shot.

The pattern shot of flying geese with their wings in similar positions looks good against a plain sky. There is the added touch in this photograph with the lone Canada goose joining the snow geese, something that one rarely sees. (300mm f/2.8 lens)

Restricting the number of colors in the background helps unify the composition. Instead of taking the bird against a background of mixed green and brown tones, select one color for the background and coax the bird into that background or wait for him to move there. Note the difference between the two portrait shots of wood ducks. The one on the left has the duck well focused with good color, but the mixed background detracts from the duck. The duck on the right is immediately more pleasing because of the simpler blue background.

Another approach to simplifying the composition is to have no background at all in the shot. A cloudless blue sky, plain blue water, a foggy or white sky all emphasize the birds themselves. With a plain background, there must be enough interest in the behavior or the pattern of the birds to carry the composition. The pattern shot of the flying geese with their wings in the same position looks good against a plain sky. There is a little added touch to this photograph with the lone Canada goose joining the flock of snow geese—something that one rarely sees.

The golden sidelighting of the late afternoon sun transforms "Geese in the Marsh" into a delicate tapestry of rich, harmonious colors seen against a neutral pale-gray water. (300mm f/4.5 lens)

7 / Color and Light in Waterfowl Photography

When using color films, it is important to remember that color itself is an integral part of the composition. An understanding of color and light as design elements adds to the photographer's ability to create more artistic presentations of the subject. For a lucid discussion of color theory as applied to general photography, I recommend the book *Color Design in Photography* by Harold Mante. The book discusses color theory in some detail and illustrates how colors affect one another and the viewer. In this chapter, we will touch upon a few of the ways the waterfowl photographer can control color through careful attention to lighting and through adding color with environmental surroundings.

Color as an Element in Design

Painters are very much aware of color as they work on a painting, mixing pigments into an infinite variety of shades and juxtaposing one color with another at will. Photographers, on the other hand, often take color for granted, failing to see that there are possibilities for manipulating the colors of nature to produce more creative compositions. Without using colored filters of any sort, the photographer can greatly alter the appearance of a photograph by thoughtful use of natural light. One can also add color to the composition by incorporating color from flowers, leaves, sky reflections, grasses, and trees. Even with the most interesting subject matter very artistically arranged, if the color is poor, the photograph suffers.

Color often makes or breaks a photograph. Good color rendition can make what would otherwise be an ordinary photograph into something special. Imagine, for example, a marsh scene with geese feeding in the grasses and swimming on the water. This scene can easily by found and photographed at different times in the day. At some hours of the day, the scene will appear dull and uninteresting, while at certain other times the same scene may provide a colorful, vibrant, and attractive photograph. The setting and the birds might be exactly the same, but in one case the photograph would not be worth a second glance, while in another case it might be a prize winner. All the compositional elements except for the lighting would be the same. It is the lighting and therefore the color that changes, and it is the color that determines our response to the photograph in this example.

The photograph titled "Geese in the Marsh" is an example of the scene described above. Had this photograph been taken at midday instead of just before sunset, there would have been no interest to this scene at all. In midday, the colors would have been entirely different—a mix of browns, greens, blue sky reflections from the water, plus the gray and brown tones of the geese themselves. However, with the golden sidelighting of the late afternoon sun, the whole scene is transformed into a harmonious and limited range of colors seen against neutral pale grey water. There are no distracting blues or green in this scene, only golds, deep orange, browns, tans, and black and white. The unified background coloring complements the brown tones of the geese. Their dark heads stand out against the neutral pale gray sky reflection in the water.

Photographs such as "Geese in the Marsh" do not generally happen by accident. They are carefully planned in terms of the time of day chosen for shooting and the angle and direction of the sunlight relative to the photographer and the subject. By thinking ahead of time about what you wish to communicate in a given photograph, you can de-

Overcast or bright but cloudy days produce a neutral color when reflected off water. The conditions allow a restricted range of colors in photography, often with pleasing results. This scene would be less effective with blue water. (400mm f/3.5 lens with 1.4x teleconverter)

cide what type of lighting and color would best support or convey the message. Of course it isn't always possible to find just the combination of desired background, proper lighting and coloring, and cooperative waterfowl for your photography. But it is surprising how often you can find what you are looking for when you know where to find the birds.

Limiting the range of colors often enhances a composition. The color range will be limited when there is only one primary color plus the blends made from that primary color. In the case of "Geese in the Marsh," the primary color yellow was accompanied by the secondary color made from the combination of yellow and red-orange and the tertiary colors made from mixing orange with blue-brown. In "Geese in the Marsh" the blue-green-violet part of the spectrum is virtually absent. The colors are all muted or mixed versions of the yellow, orange, and brown part of the color spectrum. The richness of the color is accentuated by the soft golden sidelighting that casts a golden hue over the entire scene.

Choosing to photograph on a day with clouded but bright sky light will automatically eliminate

blue from the sky and water reflections, leaving a neutral color instead. Foggy days do the same thing. In both cases the contrast will be reduced as shadows are eliminated without direct sunlight. With an overcast or clouded sky you can achieve a totally white background for either flying birds or birds on the water. With a white or pale-gray background, the coloring of the birds themselves will be much more apparent to the viewer. Subtle color differences will be more visible in the softer diffuse lighting of a clouded day. The scene of the geese at the water's edge is an example of the kind of coloring one can find on overcast days.

Other possibilities for limiting the number of colors in a composition include shooting against a unified color background, such as green leaves or grasses, brown reeds and grasses, or, of course, all-blue water or sky. Compositions with a large mass of one background color against which a smaller spot of contrasting color is seen are often very effective. For example, a brilliant red cardinal photographed against a larger area of green leaves with no other color in the scene would have much more impact than the same cardinal shown against a multi-colored background. In this example, the red would be contrasted with its complementary color opposite—green. Juxtaposing two complementary colors in the composition (red/green, yellow/violet, blue/orange) in proper proportion and balance to one another makes a pleasing composition.

Within the world of waterfowl, it is difficult to find true complementary color opposites for strong color contrast. A yellow duckling shown against blue-violet water (yellow/violet being a primary complementary pair of colors) is one of the few examples I can think of. Usually such strong color contrasts are not found with ducks and geese in their natural environments.

However, you can sometimes limit the photograph to two or three colors by careful choice of background. The photograph of the baby goslings was taken through green leaves to the geese in the green grass. Here the small yellow goslings stand out against the mass of green surroundings, emphasizing their diminutive size in relation to the plants around them. The unified green background adds to the impact of this shot.

The sleeping snow geese are another example of a composition with a limited number of colors. Here the white and blue-gray feathers of the geese bodies are contrasted against a dark-blue sky reflected off the ice. There is a small amount of contrasting pink and rosy-brown in the feet and cheeks of the geese. The deep-blue color was the result of slight underexposure in strong sidelighting. This shot was taken shortly after sunrise.

In photographs with more than two or three colors, it is still possible to achieve color unity by paying attention to the relative amounts of each color in the scene. A scene with five or six colors, each with roughly the same mass, and no one color predominating, would look rather confusing to the eye. On the other hand, another photograph with six colors, in which one or two colors clearly dominate the scene through the relative size of the areas they cover, might be a very good composition.

In the scene of the three wood ducks on a log, the largest areas of color are from the greens in the water. The next largest area of color is the blue-grey of the log and its reflection, a color that is repeated in some of the ducks' feathers. The remaining colors of reds, maroon, green, and white all occupy much smaller areas in the photograph. There is a unity to the color here because of the relative sizes of the color masses. The bright color in the upper left corner is somewhat distracting. It came from out-of-focus leaves on the nearby bank.

Simplifying the photograph by limiting the range of colors in it often increases its impact. Here the small yellow goslings stand out against the mass of green, emphasizing their diminutive size in relation to the plants around them. (400mm f/3.5 lens)

The shot of sleeping snow geese, taken shortly after sunrise, is another example of a composition with a limited range of colors. (400mm f/3.5 lens)

Color unity and balance can still be achieved in photographs with five or six colors when one or two colors clearly are dominant due to their relative mass in the composition. The greens and blue-grays occupy the most space in this shot of preening wood ducks, while the areas of the brighter colors are much smaller. (300mm f/2.8 lens)

Canada geese flying to sunset. When waterfowl take off from the ground or water, they fly into the wind just like airplanes. It is helpful to be able to predict where your subjects will fly to obtain shots like this one. (400mm f/3.5 lens)

Adding Color to Photographs

Sometimes the addition of color to a photograph will liven up an otherwise pedestrian composition. There are several techniques for adding color to waterfowl photographs. One of the easiest, of course, is to take the birds silhouetted against a vibrantly colored sky. A few clouds at sunrise or sunset offer the best possibilities for brilliant color. With the proper sky, the next problem is finding a place where you can position yourself behind the birds as they fly into the color. By planning ahead of time, and looking for the most likely spots in wildlife refuges, you can be set up and prepared to shoot when the lighting is right. When I visit a new refuge, I always look over the possibilities for sunrise or sunset shots of flying birds, deciding well ahead of time where the best location for shooting will be.

The photograph below of the geese flying into the sunset was a serendipitous shot. Driving down the road in the late afternoon, I noticed the dramatic sky as I passed a field of feeding geese. I knew that sooner or later some of them would fly off, most likely taking off into the wind. I parked my car on past the geese, so that they would be between my lens and the sun as they took off. And sure enough, it was not long before several geese did just what I had hoped for, producing this shot below.

Other ways to add color to your waterfowl shots include the use of various background or foreground elements such as brightly colored fall foliage or bright flowers. In the very early fall, it is sometimes possible to photograph geese against a bank of wildflowers, as in this scene of the Canada with black-eyed Susans in the background.

The scenic shot with the brilliant fall foliage and the resting Canada geese was taken the first week the geese had returned from their migration. It was a stroke of luck to find the geese resting near the trees. Fortunately the wind was calm, so the color of the trees was reflected in the water.

Reflected fall foliage can also make a brilliant

Adding color to waterfowl scenic photographs is easy when fall flowers are in bloom. (300mm f/3.5 lens)

The bright fall foliage and its reflection in the quiet water are what make this photograph special. "Journey's end" shows Canada geese resting after their long fall migration. (180mm f/2.8 lens)

Leaf reflections add color to this shot of a wood duck.

background for photographing waterfowl. Golden or red reflections are especially good background color for shots of Canada geese and other birds with dark feathers. The photograph of the female wood duck is a good example of color added through the use of leaf reflections.

Another approach to using fall foliage for color in waterfowl photographs involves shooting through a thin line of leaves to the birds beyond. The golden background of this wood duck photograph was the result of such a shot, taken on a windy day. In this type of photography, be prepared to waste a lot of film! Focus on the duck, ignoring the foreground elements, and press the shutter when you think the subject can be seen clearly through the foreground. Set your exposure compensation for the fore-

ground elements rather than the background. The camera meter will read the bright leaves waving in front of the subject more than the duck behind. Because of the bright yellow leaves, I opened up ⅔ of a stop for this scene.

Light and Exposure

It is the light—both the amount of light and the type of light—that determines proper exposure for a given film. The amount of light can be measured with a light meter, provided one understands the limitations of light meters. The comments below apply equally to hand-held meters and to in-camera light meters.

Most light meters are calibrated to read all colors as though they were midrange colors similar in

The soft, romantic mood of this wood duck came from shooting him through a thin line of yellow leaves. (300mm f/2.8 lens)

tone to the 18% reflectance gray card. With midrange colors such as gray tree trunks or green grass, the light meter readings will be accurate. Therefore, with these midtone colors, the light meter readings can be used directly to set the camera exposures.

With colors lighter or darker than midrange tones—that is, colors approaching white or black in tone, such as a pale-yellow flower or a dark-brown dog—the light meter will not be accurate. It will read both the light and the dark colors as though they were midrange tones. The light colors will therefore be too dark and the darks too light if you use the meter reading directly without making any adjustments or compensations. In order to use the light meter for accurate exposure, it is necessary to learn a few rules for making adjustments to the meter readings with light and with dark colors.

Correct exposure is essential to good color rendition. Slide films are especially unforgiving of improper exposure. Color print films have a little more tolerance for poor exposure. With a little practice and a few rules for making compensation to the meter readings, you should be able to master proper exposure for color films.

For a more complete in-depth explanation of exposure, see the fine article by Larry West in *Birder's World*, or the book by John Shaw, *The Nature Photographer's Complete Guide to Professional Field Techniques*.

General Guidelines for Meter Compensations—Light and Dark Tones

I. Under Average Lighting Conditions:

Situation	Exposure Compensation
Subject has both very light and very dark colors	Add ⅓ to ⅔ stop, depending on brightness of light areas to expose for detail in light areas: If necessary, sacrifice detail in dark areas.
Subject is lighter than midrange tone	Add ⅓ to ⅔ stop.
Subject is nearly white in low to average lighting	Add ⅔ to 1⅓ stop.
Subject is a little darker than midrange tone	Subtract ⅓ to ⅔ stop.
Subject is dark brown	Subtract ⅓ to ⅔ stop.
Small subject is seen against very dark background	Subtract ⅓ to ⅔ stop (meter will read background).
Small subject is seen against very bright blue, like water or sky	Add ⅓ stop.
Small subject is seen against light-gray or almost-white background, like cloudy sky or gray reflected water	Add ⅔ to 1⅓ stop.
Subject is seen against bright pale tones of dry grass—tan-yellow or whitish	Add ⅓ to ⅔ stop.
Small subject is seen against bright snow	Add 1 to 2 stops.

II. Under Unusual Lighting Conditions:

Condition of Light	Exposure Compensation
Bright midday sunlight	Add ⅓ stop.
High altitude (5,000 feet or more) bright light	Add ⅓ to ⅔ stop.
Heavy fog—diffuse light	Add ⅔ to 1⅓ stops depending on brightness of sun coming through.
Cloudy day on land	Add ⅓ stop.
Cloudy day light reflected off water	Add ⅔ to 1⅓ stops.

Meter Calibration

Before applying the general rules for compensation with light meters, it is important to verify whether your light meter does indeed read midrange tones as midrange tones. Many meters are calibrated to this standard, but many others are not. To be sure of accurate readings, you need to calibrate your light meter to read midrange tones properly if it does not already do so. One procedure for calibrating light meters recommended by West and Shaw involves the sunny f/16 rule, as they have named it. On a sunny day at midday with the light coming from behind over your shoulder, point your camera meter at green grass or, for more accuracy, an 18% reflectance gray card. In bright sunlight this midrange tone should call for an exposure reading of f/16 at 1/60 second for Kodachrome 64 film. For whatever speed of film you are using, set the ISO dial (ASA dial) for the film loaded. Then manually choose a shutter speed that is closest to the ISO number of the film. For example, for K64, 1/60 second; for Ektachrome 100 or Fujichrome 100, 1/125 second; for K200, 1/250 second; and so on.

Since we know that the proper exposure or f-stop for the sunny midrange tone with ISO film exposed for 1/60 second is f/16, you can check the calibration of your light meter by seeing what f-stop it reads. If you are using a built-in camera light meter, set the focal distance to infinity, and with the sun behind you point the lens at the 18% reflectance grey card or green grass. What does the light meter indicate on the f-stop scale? If it reads anything other than f/16 at the shutter speed closest to the ISO film number, your meter is NOT calibrated to read midrange tones correctly.

In the event your meter reads something other than f/16, move the ISO dial until the meter does read f/16. Then look at the number on the ISO dial. Write it down and remember that this number on the ISO dial is what you need for this particular camera meter with film this speed. Make the same calibration test using the sunny f/16 rule with all the speeds of film you use. If you always remember to make the compensating change to the ISO dial with your varied film speeds, you will have a meter that is reliably calibrated to read midrange tones properly. You can then use your meter readings directly to set exposures for midrange colors. This calibration will also give you a standard point for making adjustments to light meter readings for very light or very dark tones.

Fog and Heavy Haze

Fog or heavy haze provides an opportunity for some unusual and sometimes very delicate and beautiful photographs. Fog diffuses the light, softens edges, and mutes colors. Scenic or medium-range photographs are particularly effective in fog. The light is deceptive in fog . . . it is really much brighter than it may seem. Care must be taken to avoid underexposing fog scenes. The brightness and delicate effect are lost if the slide is underexposed. If I am metering medium-toned subjects and background in fog, I will open up a minimum of ⅓ stop, sometimes ⅔ stop or a whole stop, depending on how much sunlight is coming through the fog. If my meter is reading foggy sky or water reflected off foggy gray sky, I will open up ⅔ to 1⅓ stops beyond what my light meter reads.

Tundra Swans Flying In. Backlighted subjects sometimes are more dramatic and interesting than subjects with frontal lighting.

8 / Printing, Matting, and Framing

Prints from Slides

If you want really good quality prints from your favorite slides, then you must either print them yourself or use a custom laboratory. All my slides are developed by Kodak, including the Fujichrome and Ektachrome slides. They offer consistent, reliable developing for slides. Prints from Kodak, however, may or may not be satisfactory. That is why most of the photographers who sell prints at waterfowl shows use custom laboratories if they do not do their own printing.

There are two choices in custom printing: Cibachrome prints made directly from the 35mm slide, and Type C prints made from internegatives. (The internegative is usually a 4 x 5-inch negative made by photographing the slide. The print is made from the internegative.) Since the costs for two or three copies of one print are roughly the same for both processes, the decision about which type of print can be made primarily on the basis of your preferences and/or the characteristic of the slide you have chosen to print. Both types of prints have advantages and disadvantages.

The Cibachrome print has very vibrant color, especially the reds, yellows, and oranges. The darks, especially black, come out a little deeper in tone in Cibachrome than the darks on an internegative print. The deeper-toned darks give the Cibachrome print a distinctive appearance that sometimes really enhances the appearance of a photograph. Cibachrome prints have a clarity and vibrance that sets them apart from other prints. Cibachrome prints are made on glossy or matte-finished plastic paper that has a very delicate surface, so great care must be exercised in handling these prints to avoid fingerprints, dust, and such. My printer uses a white cotton glove to handle them.

Cibachrome prints have somewhat of an advantage over prints from internegatives in terms of their life expectancy. The colors in the Cibachrome print should remain fresh and clear for a lifetime or longer. However, neither Cibachrome prints nor Type C prints can withstand being hung in direct sunlight.

Because the Cibachrome print is made directly from the slide, it tends to have a bit sharper focus than prints made from an internegative. This can be an important consideration when printing your slide in sizes as large as 20 x 24 inches or more. In smaller-sized prints such as 11 x 14, the difference in sharpness would be much less noticeable.

Prints made from internegatives tend to show better detail, especially in the dark areas. The look of these prints will be softer, more romantic in tone than the Cibachrome prints. The reds, yellows, and oranges do not jump out in prints from internegatives. If a slide is a little underexposed, it will probably print more satisfactorily with an internegative. If detail is not to be lost in a Cibachrome print, the exposure of the slide must be just right. Cibachrome will print a little darker than the slide looks in the shadow areas. This shift toward a darker print can be a problem with underexposed slides.

If I have any rule of thumb to use in choosing which type of print I make from my waterfowl slides, it is the exposure of the slide. Any underexposure at all will lead me to choose an internegative print. A second rule of thumb is whether there are bright red or yellow tones I wish to emphasize. A third consideration is whether or not this particular slide will look better with darker blacks and deep colors. When I think darker blacks will enrich the appearance, I choose Cibachrome prints. If, on the other hand, I want a softer image or one looking more like a painting, I choose prints from an internegative.

Matting your Photographic Prints

Choosing appropriate matting for your prints is essential to an artistic presentation of your work. White matting in either single or double mats is always acceptable for photographs. The white color should match any whites in the photograph. Often, however, white is not the best choice for matting colored photographs. Trying out sample mats of different colors will give you a good idea about how a given photograph will look in white versus colored matting.

Colored matting must be very carefully chosen to match colors already in the photograph. For example, with a photograph of a duck on blue water, a white mat produces a very sharply defined edge to the picture. It may not look as good as a matching blue mat. Blue matting for a photograph with blue sky or water as the predominant background color seems to continue the picture beyond its borders. It is essential, however, in working with blues that the particular tone of the blue match the blue of the print. A nonmatching blue detracts from the final effect of the photograph. When blue would be the best color and I cannot find a matching blue, I usually resort to white matting.

When green is the predominate background color, there is a little more leeway for choosing the mat color than there is with blue backgrounds. Often the green tones vary in the photograph, allowing the use of several different shades of green matting. In this case, experimentation with sample matting allows one to choose the best green for the particular photograph. Sometimes a nonmatching green complements the green tones in the picture rather than detracts from them.

With photographs containing scenery, the choice of colors for matting increases. With dry fields, grass, and reeds in the background, there are many colors from which to choose matching matting. Usually the outer mat looks good in a pale neutral color such as beige, tan, cream, or pale gray. With a photograph showing brown and tan grasses, for example, a pale tone of beige for the outer mat with a darker tone of brown for the 1/8-inch inner mat might go well together. The color selected for the inner mat should complement both the colors in the photograph and in the outer mat. The inner mat color may be an accent color that you wish to emphasize in the photograph. It may also be a darker tone of the same color used for the outer mat, for example, light brown for the outer mat and a darker tone of the same brown for the inner mat.

Generally, matting colors should be fairly neutral. Vivid colors like yellow, red, orange, lavender, or gold would compete with the photograph for attention. The eye should not be drawn to the matting or framing but to the picture. The matting and framing simply provide the setting for the photograph.

A recent addition to the range of available matting is the black core mat. This mat board has black instead of white edges at the cut, making it an ideal choice where you wish to emphasize blacks in the photograph. Black core acid-free matting by Crescent is now available in twenty-six colors, including several silk textures. Bainbridge also makes an acid-free black core mat board, offering forty color choices. When plain white matting is the best choice, a black core white mat may look better than the white core mats.

There are two types of matting to consider: acid-free matting and regular matting. The acid-free mat is a little more expensive than the plain paper matting. Acid-free matting will not fade or bleed with age, but the plain paper matting will fade out in a few years. When matting Cibachrome photographs, I use only acid-free matting because of the longer life expectancy of the Cibachrome print. If the best color is available only in the plain paper matting, it can be lined with acid-free matting underneath to protect the photograph. Since the black core mat board is nearly acid-free, there is no worry about deterioration with it.

Framing

Framing for photographs must be just as carefully chosen as the matting. Too wide a frame will overpower the photograph. Usually a fairly narrow frame in wood or metal that picks up one of the colors in the print looks best. The matting and frame must go well together, and both should contribute to the overall effect of the photograph.

Wood frames add a distinctive appearance to photographs and are a good choice if the piece is to be hung in a room with traditional furnishings. Metal framing might be a better choice if the photograph will be hung in a modernistic setting, with chrome and glass, for example. Wooden frames must be thin and light enough that they do not draw attention away from the photo. Ornate, wide, or heavy frames are not a good choice for photographs. Rounded, as opposed to flat, frames accentuate the rounded duck and goose bodies.

Metal framing comes in a wide range of colors and a dozen different styles. Again, the metal frames should not be too wide. The metal frames are very easy to assemble and take apart again if you wish to change the photograph at a later date. Care must be taken in storing and transporting pictures with metal frames because these frames scratch very easily and there is no way to remove the scratches. The metallic metal surfaces are more durable than the painted metal frames.

Backing for the Photograph

The best backing on which to mount your photograph is acid-free foam core. Being a plastic material, it will not absorb moisture, nor will it bend eas-ily. It is more durable than cardboard and will not disintegrate with time.

There are several ways to attach your photo to the backing. Dry mounting is fine for Type C internegative prints if you wish to do that. But dry mounting is *not* recommended for Cibachrome prints. Instead, Cibachrome prints should be hung from the top with thin linen tape hinges, or a special photo adhesive should be used. Be sure that the tape hinge does not extend below the area covered by the matting or it will produce a bulge in the picture that is visible. The plastic paper of the Cibachrome print is very thin and delicate. Dust should be air blown, not brushed, off the print to avoid scratching the surface.

The out of focus foreground elements add a little interest and depth to this redhead duck shot.

9 / Selling Waterfowl Photography

Waterfowl and Wildlife Art Shows

Wildlife art shows have been springing up all over the country in the past couple of years. There are now major shows in the West, the Midwest, the South, and the East as interest in wildlife art continues to grow. Most of these shows, however, do not feature photography. Many of them have not had any photographers exhibiting and selling their work. Nonetheless, the future looks brighter as a few of the more important shows are adding photographers to their list of exhibitors. Several of the largest waterfowl-oriented shows have had photography exhibits from the beginning, notably the Easton (Maryland) Waterfowl Festival, the Mid-Atlantic Wildfowl Show in Virginia Beach, Virginia, and the Northeastern Wildlife Exposition in Albany, New York. The Southeastern Wildlife Exposition also has had photography exhibitors in the past few years.

The wildlife and waterfowl shows vary greatly in numbers of exhibitors and visitors. The Easton Festival draws more than 20,000 visitors to the three-day show. This show has had twenty or more excellent waterfowl photographers exhibiting in the show each year. Exhibiting in the Easton Waterfowl Festival is limited to the very best photographers. This festival has the best record of all the shows for sales of photography.

The Mid-Atlantic Wildfowl Festival in Virginia Beach, Virginia, is much smaller than the Easton show, with fewer visitors, but it is a quality show in a fine exhibition hall. There are a number of good photographers exhibiting each year at this show. It features a friendly photography contest that takes place during the show. Judges visit each photographer's display, selecting those photographs they consider the most artistic for ribbons that are awarded during the show.

The Southeastern and Northeastern Wildlife Expositions each welcome photographers as exhibitors in their show. The Southeastern Exposition is a very large show, with exhibits in a number of buildings around the center of Charleston, South Carolina. It drew more than 42,000 visitors in 1988. However, the public attending the Southeastern Expo does not seem to buy photographs nearly to the extent that visitors to the Easton Waterfowl Festival do. The Northeastern Wildlife Exposition in its present format, with artists, carvers, sculptors, and photographers, was first held in 1987 in Albany, New York. Since this is such a new show, it is difficult to predict how well photographs will sell there in the future. (See reference list for addresses on these shows.)

The wildlife art shows also differ in their sponsorship. Some are sponsored by conservation organizations that donate the profits to wildlife conservation. Others are more commercial ventures. Still others are sponsored as fund-raising efforts for schools or other nonprofit organizations.

It is hard to keep up with all of the new wildlife art shows being organized each year. The best resource for information about dates and addresses of wildlife art shows in the calendar of events page in *Wildlife Art News*. This beautiful and informative magazine is published six times a year. It features articles about artists, their art forms, and the artists' views on wildlife art, and frequently an article on photography. The editor, Robert Koenke, plans to add more features about wildlife photography in the next year or two, including an occasional profile of a wildlife photographer. *Wildlife Art News* lists the major wildlife art shows for the succeeding three months with dates and addresses to write to for information. A review of back issues will provide information for contacting these annual shows where you might exhibit. The lead time for entering most of the shows in nine months to a year.

Waterfowl and wildlife art shows offer the opportunity to exhibit your framed prints where the public can see them. Selling matted prints and framed photographs is also possible at most of these shows. However, I must caution photographers new to these shows that they cannot expect to make much money this way. The art-buying public is far more interested in buying paintings and prints of paintings than in buying photography. Very few photographers make money selling prints at these shows. The costs of producing, matting, and framing the prints, and the expenses of entering the show leave little margin for profit at the prices that most of the exhibitors can sell their prints for. Furthermore, it is not easy to predict just which photographs ill appeal the most to potential buyers. A shot that you really like may or may not sell that well. Colorful sunsets with ducks and geese, and cute baby ducks and geese sometimes sell well. Hunters like flying birds and scenes typical of what they see out hunting, while other people seem to buy more romantic, dreamy types of photographs. Attractive hunting dogs and puppies may also sell at waterfowl shows, though one sometimes hears the comment, "That looks just like Blackie! Isn't he adorable?" But because it isn't Blackie, they don't buy it!

Selling Slides to Magazines and Book Publishers

There are several excellent resources for information about potential buyers for your waterfowl slides. Three of them are *Photographer's Market: Where and How to Sell Your Photographs*, an annual publication; *The Guilfoyle Report*, a quarterly newsletter for nature photographers; and *Photoletter*, published by PhotoSource, a monthly newsletter. All of these publications give addresses and descriptions of the types of coverage sought by magazine, book, calendar, and paper goods publishers. The *Photographer's Market* is a general photography publication, listing overall subject needs, terms, and submission guidelines. *The Guilfoyle Report* is tailored specifically to the nature and wildlife photographer. It includes articles on the latest equipment, films, places to visit for good photographs, and marketing news. For the photographer seriously interested in selling nature slides to publications, *The Guilfoyle Report* is well worth the $48

annual cost. PhotoSource's *Photoletter* lists buyers' specific subject and picture needs, deadlines, and payment offered. For the serious photographer, PhotoSource has two more publications, one weekly and the other twice-monthly, that list specific photo needs with tight deadlines. (See reference list for addresses of these publications.)

When sending out slides to publishers, it is important that your name and the copyright symbol be on each slide, usually on the smaller sides of the slides. Many people purchase a rubber stamp with the copyright symbol and their name beside it. Also, the top of the slide should be captioned to identify the main subject. Many buyers want both common and Latin names, and where the slide was taken noted on the slide. Each slide should be protected with a protective 2' x 2' sleeve—a plastic clear covering that fits over the slide. The covered slides should then be placed in an acid-free page holding twenty 2' x 2' slides. Both of these items can be purchased at any comprehensive photographic supply store.

Photographers who wish to sell their slides to book, magazine, or calendar publishers must be prepared for lots of rejection. The competition is fierce and the buyers are somewhat unpredictable. Your rejected photographs might be just as good as, or even better than, those chosen for publication, but they might not have quite the angle, the color, the nuance, that the editor is looking for. And one editor may reject a slide that another will snap up. Furthermore, there is a limited market for slides of waterfowl. There seem to be many more publications using slides of small birds than there are publishing photographs of waterfowl. There are several magazines devoted to waterfowl hunting, but they do not pay well for photographs. If you can tolerate many rejection notices and low payment for your photographs, and if you have top quality, tack-sharp slides, you may be successful in getting your work into print.

Among the magazines that offer possibilities for selling your slides are *Birder's World*, *Gray's Sporting Journal*, Wildfowl, and the *Living Bird Quarterly*. Once in a while *Audubon Magazine*, *National Geographic*, and the National Wildlife Federation magazines (*National Wildlife*, *International Wildlife*, and *Ranger Rick* magazine) publish individual photographs or stories on waterfowl. (Addresses for some of these magazines are listed in the references at the end of this chapter.)

Ducks Unlimited and *Waterfowl* are member magazines for nonprofit corporations and showcases for your work. *Ducks Unlimited* recently began to offer payment, although the latter, because of their nonprofit nature, cannot pay for the use of your photographs. Both of these organizations donate the money they raise to the conservation of waterfowl. Therefore, when you contribute the use of your photographs to them, you are making a direct contribution to help the ducks.

Lastly, the waterfowl photographer's market is not limited to United States' publications and advertising opportunities. The market is an international one, with buyers to be found from Asia to Europe, the United Kingdom to Canada.

This tail-up mallard was feeding among the grasses on the river bottom. (400mm f/3.5 lens)

Major Waterfowl Shows

Easton, Maryland
Photography
The Waterfowl Festival
P.O. Box 929
Easton, Maryland 21601

Mid-Atlantic Wildfowl Show
c/o Dr. John Krueger
1424 Laurel View Drive
Virginia Beach, Virginia 23451

Northeastern Wildlife Exposition
8 Wade Road
Latham, New York 12110

Southeastern Wildlife Exposition
237 King Street
Charleston, South Carolina 29401

Magazines

Audubon Magazine
950 Third Avenue
New York, New York 10022

Birder's World
720 E. 8th Street
Holland, Michigan 49423

Bird Watching
Bretton Court
Bretton, Peterborough PE3 8DZ
England

British Birds
Fountains
Park Lane
Blunham, Bedford MK44 3NJ
England

BBC Wildlife
Broadcasting House
Whiteladies Road
Bristol BS8 2LR
England

Ducks Unlimited Magazine
1 Waterfowl Way
Long Grove, Illinois 60047

Gray's Sporting Journal
205 Willow Street
South Hamilton, Massachusetts 01982

Living Bird Quarterly
Laboratory of Ornithology at Cornell University
159 Sapsucker Woods Road
Ithaca, New York 14850

National Geographic
National Geographic Society
17th and M Streets, Northwest
Washington, D.C. 20036

National Wildlife,
International Wildlife, or
Ranger Rick
National Wildlife Federation
1400 Sixteenth Street Northwest
Washington, D.C. 20036

Waterfowl
Waterfowl U.S.A., Limited
The Waterfowl Building
P.O. Box 50
Edgefield, South Carolina 29824

Wildfowl
P.O. Box 35098
Des Moines, Iowa 50315

Wildlife Art News
3455 Dakota Avenue South
P.O. Box 16246
St. Louis Park, Minnesota 55416

World Wildlife News
World Wildlife Fund
Panda House
Weyside Park
Godalming, Surrey GU7 1XR
England

Reference List

British Trust for Ornithology, Beech Grove, Station Road, Tring, Hertfordshire, HP23 5NR, England

Chambers, Glenn D. "Makin' like a Muskrat." *Ducks Unlimited Magazine* (March/April 1987): 17-7.

Eidenier, Connie, ed. *1987 Photographer's Market: Where to Sell Your Photographs.* Cincinnati: Writer's Digest, 1986.

Findlay, J.C. *A Bird Finding Guide to Canada.* Edmonton, Alberta: Aspen, 1984.

Foott, Jeff. "Hot Tips for Cold Trips." *Outdoor Photographer* (February 1988): 44-47.

The Guilfoyle Report: A Quarterly Forum for Nature Photographers. AG Editions, Inc. 142 Bank Street, New York, N.Y. 10014.

Mante, Harold. *Color Design in Photography.* New York: Van Nostrand, 1972.

National Wildlife Rehabilitators Association, RR 1, Box 125E, Brighton, Illinois, 62012.

Nikon Handbook Series: Lenses and Lens Systems. New York: American Photographic, 1979.

Norton, Boyd. "Film Testing Update." *The Guilfoyle Report* 6 (Fall 1987): 11-12.

Photoletter. PhotoSource International. Osceola, WI. 54020

Riley, Laura and William. *Guide to the National Wildlife Refuges.* Garden City, New York: Anchor, 1979.

Royal Society for Nature Conservation, The Green Nettleham, Lincoln, LN2 2NR, England

Royal Society for the Protection of Birds, The Lodge, Sandy, Bedfordshire, SG19 2BR, England

Shaw, John. *The Nature Photographer's Complete Guide to Professional Field Techniques.* New York: American Photographic, 1984.

Wesley, David and William Leitch, eds. *Fireside Waterfowler: Fundamentals of Duck and Goose Ecology.* Harrisburg: Stackpole, 1987.

West, Larry. "Exposure-wise." *Birder's World* (July/August, 1988): 31-35.

Index